AF568141

First Published - 2011

Reprinted - 2017

ISBN: 978-81-8356-837-1

Textbook of Environmental Chemistry

Published by:

DISCOVERY PUBLISHING HOUSE PVT. LTD.

4383/4B, Ansari Road, Darya Ganj
New Delhi-110 002 (India)
Phone: +91-11-23279245, 43596064-65
Fax: +91-11-23253475
E-mail: discoverypublishinghouse@gmail.com
sales@discoverypublishinggroup.com
web: www.discoverypublishinggroup.com

Printed at:
Infinity Imaging Systems
Delhi

PREFACE

Environmental chemistry is the scientific study of the chemical and biochemical phenomena that occur in natural places. It should not be confused with green chemistry, which seeks to reduce potential pollution at its source. It can be defined as the study of the sources, reactions, transport, effects, and fates of chemical species in the air, soil, and water environments; and the effect of human activity on these. Environmental chemistry is an interdisciplinary science that includes atmospheric, aquatic and soil chemistry, as well as heavily relying on analytical chemistry and being related to environmental and other areas of science.

Environmental chemistry involves first understanding how the uncontaminated environment works, which chemicals in what concentrations are present naturally, and with what effects. Without this it would be impossible to accurately study the effects humans have on the environment through the release of chemicals.

Environmental chemists draw on a range of concepts from chemistry and various environmental sciences to assist in their study of what is happening to a chemical species in the environment. Important general concepts from chemistry include understanding chemical reactions and equations, solutions, units, sampling, and analytical techniques.

Author

Contents

INTRODUCTION

Environmental chemistry is the scientific study of the chemical and biochemical phenomena that occur in natural places. It should not be confused with green chemistry, which seeks to reduce potential pollution at its source. It can be defined as the study of the sources, reactions, transport, effects, and fates of chemical species in the air, soil, and water environments; and the effect of human activity on these. Environmental chemistry is an interdisciplinary science that includes atmospheric, aquatic and soil chemistry, as well as heavily relying on analytical chemistry and being related to environmental and other areas of science.

Environmental chemistry involves first understanding how the uncontaminated environment works, which chemicals in what concentrations are present naturally, and with what effects. Without this it would be impossible to accurately study the effects humans have on the environment through the release of chemicals.

Environmental chemists draw on a range of concepts from chemistry and various environmental sciences to assist in their study of what is happening to a chemical species in the environment. Important general concepts from chemistry include understanding chemical reactions and equations, solutions, units, sampling, and analytical techniques.

Contamination

A contaminant is a substance present in nature due to human activity, that would not otherwise be there the term contaminant is often used interchangeably with pollutant, which is a substance that has a detrimental impact on the environment it is in. Whilst a contaminant is sometimes defined as a substance present in the environment as a result of human activity, but without harmful effects, it is sometimes the case that toxic or harmful effects from contamination only become apparent at a later date.

The "medium" (e.g. soil) or organism (e.g. fish) affected by the pollutant or contaminant is called a receptor, whilst a sink is a chemical medium or species that retains and interacts with the pollutant.

Environmental Indicators

Chemical measures of water quality include dissolved oxygen (DO), chemical oxygen demand (COD), biochemical oxygen demand (BOD), total dissolved solids (TDS), pH, nutrients nitrates and phosphorus), heavy metals (including copper, zinc, cadmium, lead and mercury), and pesticides. BOD is a measure of the amount, in milligrams, of dissolved oxygen needed to break down the organic matter present in one litre of water for five days at 20 degrees Celsius[citation needed]. Pure water has a BOD of 0-3ppm (1 ppm = 1 mg/L). A BOD of 5ppm or slightly more would indicate that the water is somewhat contaminated. Thus BOD gives an idea of the extent of organic waste present in water. Sometimes, the water in the vicinity of factories is found to have a BOD as high as 1000ppm. This means that the water is highly contaminated.

Applications

Environmental chemistry is used by the Environment Agency (in England and Wales), the Environmental Protection Agency (in the United States) the Association of Public Analysts, and other environmental agencies and research bodies around the world to detect and identify the nature and source of pollutants. These can include:

- Heavy metal contamination of land by industry. These can then be transported into water bodies and be taken up by living organisms.
- Nutrients leaching from agricultural land into water courses, which can lead to algal blooms and eutrophication.
- Urban runoff of pollutants washing off impervious surfaces (roads, parking lots, and rooftops) during rain storms. Typical pollutants include gasoline, motor oil and other hydrocarbon compounds, metals, nutrients and sediment (soil).

Methods

Quantitative chemical analysis is a key part of environmental chemistry, since it provides the data that frame most environmental studies.

Common analytical techniques used for quantitative determinations in environmental chemistry include classical wet chemistry, such as gravimetric, titrimetric and electrochemical methods. More sophisticatedmatography-mass spectrometry (LC/MS). Non-MS methods using GCs and LCs having universal or specific detectors are still staples in the arsenal of available analytical tools.

Other parameters often measured in environmental chemistry are radiochemicals. These are pollutants which emit radioactive materials, such as alpha and beta particles, posing danger to human heaays and immunoassays are utilized for toxicity evaluations of chemical effects on various organisms.

2

SOIL CONTAMINATION

Soil contamination or soil pollution is caused by the presence of man-made chemicals or other alteration in the natural soil environment. This type of contamination typically arises from the rupture of underground storage tanks, application of pesticides, percolation of contaminated surface water to subsurface strata, oil and fuel dumping, leaching of wastes from landfills or direct discharge of industrial wastes to the soil. The most common chemicals involved are petroleum hydrocarbons, solvents, pesticides, lead and other heavy metals. This occurrence of this phenomenon is correlated with the degree of industrialization and intensity of chemical usage.

The concern over soil contamination stems primarily from health risks, both of direct contact and from secondary contamination of water supplies Mapping of contaminated soil sites and the resulting cleanup are time consuming and expensive tasks, requiring extensive amounts of geology, hydrology, chemistry and computer modeling skills.

It is in North America and Western Europe that the extent of contaminated land is most well known, with many of countries in these areas having a legal framework to identify and deal with this environmental problem; this however may well be just the tip of the iceberg with developing countries very likely to be the next generation of new soil contamination cases.

The immense and sustained growth of the People's Republic of China since the 1970s has exacted a price from the land in increased soil pollution. The State Environmental Protection Administration believes it to be a threat to the environment, to food safety and to sustainable agriculture. According to a scientific sampling, 150 million mi (100,000 square kilometres) of China's cultivated land have been polluted, with contaminated water being used to irrigate a further 32.5 million mi (21,670 square kilometres) and another two million mi (1,300 square kilometres) covered or destroyed by solid waste. In total, the area accounts for one-tenth of China's cultivatable land, and is mostly in economically developed areas. An estimated 12 million tonnes of grain are contaminated by heavy metals every year, causing direct losses of 20 billion yuan (US$2.57 billion).

The United States, while having some of the most widespread soil contamination, has actually been a leader in defining and implementing standards for cleanup. Other industrialized countries have a large number of contaminated sites, but lag the U.S. in executing remediation. Developing countries may be leading in the next generation of new soil contamination cases.

Each year in the U.S., thousands of sites complete soil contamination cleanup, some by using microbes that "eat up" toxic chemicals in soil, many others by simple excavation and others by more expensive high-tech soil vapor extraction or air stripping. At the same time, efforts proceed worldwide in creating and identifying new sites of soil contamination, particularly in industrial countries other than the U.S., and in developing countries which lack the money and the technology to adequately protect soil resources.

Health Effects

The major concern is that there are many sensitive land uses where people are in direct contact with soils such as residences, parks, schools and playgrounds. Other contact mechanisms include contamination of drinking water or inhalation of soil contaminants which have vaporized.

There is a very large set of health consequences from exposure to soil contamination depending on pollutant type, pathway of attack and vulnerability of the exposed population. Chromium and obsolete pesticide formulations are carcinogenic to populations. Lead is especially hazardous to young children, in which group there is a high risk of developmental damage to the brain, while to all populations kidney damage is a risk.

Chronic exposure to sufficient concentrations is known to be associated with higher incidence of leukemia .Obsolete pesticides such as mercury and cyclodienes are known to induce higher incidences of kidney damage, some irreversible; cyclodienes are linked to liver toxicity. Organophosphates and carbamates can induce a chain of responses leading to neuromuscular blockage.

Many chlorinated solvents induce liver changes, kidney changes and depression of the central nervous system. There is an entire spectrum of further health effects such as headache, nausea, physical fatigue, eye irritation and skin rash for the above cited and other chemicals.

Ecosystem Effects

Not unexpectedly, soil contaminants can have significant deleterious consequences for ecosystems. There are radical soil chemistry changes which can arise from the presence of many hazardous chemicals even at low concentration of the contaminant species. These changes can manifest in the alteration of metabolism of endemic microorganisms and arthropods resident in a given soil environment. The result can be virtual eradication of some of the primary food chain, which in turn have major consequences for predator or consumer species. Even if the chemical effect on lower life forms is small, the lower pyramid levels of the food chain may ingest alien chemicals, which normally become more concentrated for each consuming rung of the food chain. Many of these effects are now well known, such as the concentration of persistent DDT materials for avian consumers, leading to weakening of egg shells, increased chick mortality and potentially species extinction.

Effects occur to agricultural lands which have certain types of soil contamination. Contaminants typically alter plant metabolism, most commonly to reduce crop yields. This has a secondary effect upon soil conservation, since the languishing crops cannot shield the earth's soil mantle from erosion phenomena. Some of these chemical contaminants have long half-lives and in other cases derivative chemicals are formed from decay of primary soil contaminants.

REGULATORY FRAMEWORK

United States of America

Until about 1970 there was little widespread awareness of the worldwide scope of soil contamination or its health risks. In fact, areas of concern were often viewed as unusual or isolated incidents. Since then, the U.S. has established guidelines for handling hazardous waste and the cleanup of soil pollution. In 1980 the U.S. Superfund/CERCLA established strict rules on legal liability for soil contamination. Not only did CERCLA stimulate identification and cleanup of thousands of sites, but it raised awareness of property buyers and sellers to make soil pollution a focal issue of land use and management practices.

While estimates of remaining soil cleanup in the U.S. may exceed 200,000 sites, in other industrialized countries there is a lag of identification and cleanup functions. Even though their use of chemicals is lower than industrialized countries, often their controls and regulatory framework is quite weak. For example, some persistent pesticides that have been banned in the U.S. are in widespread uncontrolled use in developing countries. It is worth noting that the cost of cleaning up a soil contaminated site can range from as little as about $10,000 for a small spill, which can be simply excavated, to millions of dollars for a widespread event, especially for a chemical that is very mobile such as perchloroethylene.

China

China, an economy that regularly records double digit annual economic growth, has written some pieces of legislation to protect the environment, though it is disputed whether they are enough. Currently, given the amount of land in question (up to one-tenth of China's cultivatable land may be polluted), the degree of the pollution in specific locations is unclear, making both prevention and remedy difficult. Environmental regulations have been difficult to enforce, due in part to the early stage of development the country is in. The severity of the pollution is not known by the public or business population, and the situation is possibly worsening as a result.

United Kingdom

Generic guidance commonly used in the UK are the Soil Guideline Values published by DEFRA and the Environment Agency. These are screening values that demonstrate the minimal acceptable level of a substance. Above this there can be no assurances in terms of significant risk of harm to human health. These have been derived using the Contaminated Land Exposure Asseeement Model (CLEA UK). Certain input parameters such as Health Criteria Values, age and land use are fed into CLEA UK to obtain a probablistic output.

Guidance by the Inter Departmental Committee for the Redevelopment of Contaminated Land (ICRCL) has been formally withdrawn by the Department for Environment, Food and Rural Affairs (DEFRA), for use as a prescriptive document to determine the potential need for remediation or further assessment. Therefore, no further reference is made to these former guideline values.

Other generic guidance that exists (to put the concentration of a particular contaminant in context), includes the United States EPA Region 9 Preliminary Remediation Goals (US PRGs), the US EPA Region 3 Risk Based Concentrations (US EPA RBCs) and National Environment Protection Council of Australia Guideline on Investigation Levels in Soil and Groundwater.

However international guidance should only be used in the UK with clear justification. This is because foreign standards are usually particular to that country due to drivers such as political policy, geology, flood regime and epidemiology. It is generally accepted by UK regulators that only robust scientific methods that relate to the UK should be used.

The CLEA model published by DEFRA and the Environment Agency (EA) in March 2002 sets a framework for the appropriate assessment of risks to human health from contaminated land, as required by Part IIA of the Environmental Protection Act 1990. As part of this framework, generic Soil Guideline Values (SGVs) have currently been derived for ten contaminants to be used as "intervention values". These values should not be considered as remedial targets but values above which further detailed assessment should be considered.

Three sets of CLEA SGVs have been produced for three different land uses, namely residential (with and without plant uptake) allotments commercial/industrial.

It is intended that the SGVs replace the former ICRCL values. It should be noted that the CLEA SGVs relate to assessing chronic (long term) risks to human health and do not apply to the protection of ground workers during construction, or other potential receptors such as groundwater, buildings, plants or other ecosystems. The CLEA SGVs are not directly applicable to a site completely covered in hardstanding, as there is no direct exposure route to contaminated soils.

To date, the first ten of fifty-five contaminant SGVs have been published, for the following: arsenic, cadmium, chromium, lead, inorganic mercury, nickel, selenium ethyl benzene, phenol and toluene. Draft SGVs for benzene, naphthalene and xylene have been produced but their publication is on hold. Toxicological data (Tox) has been published for each of these contaminants as well as for benzo pyrene, benzene, dioxins, furans and dioxin-like PCBs, naphthalene, vinyl chloride, 1, 1, 2, 2 tetrachloroethane and 1, 1, 1, 2 tetrachloroethane, 1, 1, 1 trichloroethane, tetrachloroethene, carbon tetrachloride, 1, 2-dichloroethane, trichloroethene and xylene. The SGVs for ethyl benzene, phenol and toluene are dependent on the soil organic matter (SOM) content (which can be calculated from the total organic carbon (TOC) content). As an initial screen the SGVs for 1% SOM are considered to be appropriate.

Cleanup Options

Cleanup or remediation is analyzed by environmental scientists who utilize field measurement of soil chemicals and also apply computer models for analyzing transport and fate of soil chemicals. Thousands of soil contamination cases are currently in active cleanup across the U.S. as of 2006. There are several principal strategies for remediation.

- Excavate soil and take it to a disposal site away from ready pathways for human or sensitive ecosystem contact. This technique also applies to dredging of bay muds containing toxins.
- Aeration of soils at the contaminated site (with attendant risk of creating air pollution).

- Thermal remediation by introduction of heat to raise subsurface temperatures sufficiently high to volatize chemical contaminants out of the soil for vapour extraction. Technologies include ISTD, electrical resistance heating (ERH), and ET-DSPtm.
- Bioremediation, involving microbial digestion of certain organic chemicals. Techniques used in bioremediation include landfarming, biostimulation and bio-augmentating soil biota with commercially available microflora.
- Extraction of groundwater or soil vapor with an active electromechanical system, with subsequent stripping of the contaminants from the extract.
- Containment of the soil contaminants (such as by capping or paving over in place).
- Phytoremediation, or using plants (such as willow) to extract heavy metals.

LAND POLLUTION

Land Pollution is the degradation of earth's land surfaces often caused by human activities and their misuse of land resources. Haphazard disposal of urban and industrial wastes, exploitation of minerals, and improper use of soil by inadequate agricultural practices are a few factors. Urbanization and industrialisation are major causes of land pollution.

The Industrial Revolution set a series of events into motion which destroyed natural habitats and polluted the environment, causing diseases in both humans and animals.

Increased Mechanization

In some areas, metal ores are extracted from the ground, melted, cast and cooled using river water, which raises the temperature of water in rivers. This reduces the oxygen carrying capacity of the water and affects the aquatic life forms. The excavation of minerals leads to a large scale quarrying and defacing of land. To a large extent, this has been stopped or is more controlled, and attempts have been made to use the quarries profitably e.g. sand pits have been turned into boating lochs and some have been used as landfills. Central Scotland bears the scars of years of coal mining, with pit binges and slag heaps visible from the motorways.

The increase in the concentration of population in cities, along with the internal combustion engine, led to the increased number of roads and all the infra structure that goes with them. Roads cause visual, noise, light, air and water pollution, in addition to land pollution. The visual and noise areas are obvious, however light pollution is becoming more widely recognised as a problem. From outer space, large cities can be picked out at night by the glow of their lighting, so city dwellers seldom experience total darkness.

The contribution of vehicular traffic to air pollution is dealt with in another article, but, suffice to say that sulfur dioxide, nitrogen oxide and carbon monoxide are the main culprits. Water pollution is caused by the run off from roads of oil, salt and rubber residue, which enter the water courses and may make conditions unsuitable for certain organisms to live.

As the demand for food has grown very high, there is an increase in field size and mechanization. The increase in field size makes it economically viable for the farmer but results in loss of habitat and shelter for wildlife, as hedgerows and copses disappear. When crops are harvested, the naked soil is left open to wind after the heavy machinery has compacted it. Another consequence of more intensive agriculture is the move to monoculture. This is unnatural, it depletes the soil of nutrients, allows diseases and pests to spread and, in short, brings into play the use of chemical substances foreign to the environment.

Pesticides

Pesticides are chemicals used to kill pests and all other insects which are dangerous to human beings. These can cause soil contamination and water contamination as well. Pesticides are the chemical used for spaying to the crop. It kills the insects near by the crop which affects the crop. The biggest drawback of the pesticide is that after a certain period of time the fertility of land goes away.

Herbicides

Herbicides are used to kill weeds, especially on pavements and railways. They are similar to auxins and most are biodegradable by soil bacteria. However one group derived from trinitrophenol (2:4 D and 2:4:5 T) have the impurity dioxin, which is very toxic and causes fatality even in low concentrations. It also causes spontaneous abortions, haemorrhaging and cancer. Agent Orange (50% 2:4:5 T) was used as a defoliant in Vietnam. Eleven million gallons were used and children born since then to American soldiers who served in this conflict, have shown increased physical and mental disabilities compared to the rest of the population. It affects the head of the sperm and the chromosomes inside it.

Another herbicide, much loved by murder story writers, is Paraquat. It is highly toxic but it rapidly degrades in soil due to the action of bacteria and does not kill soil fauna.

Insecticides

Insecticides are used to rid farms of pests which damage crops. The insects damage not only standing crops but also stored ones and in the tropics it is reckoned that one third of the total production is lost during food storage. As with fungicides, the first insecticides used in the nineteenth century were inorganic e.g. Paris Green and other compounds of arsenic. Nicotine has also been used since the late eighteenth century. There are now two main groups of synthetic insecticides.

Organochlorines

Organochlorines include DDT, Aldrin, Dieldrin and BHC. They are cheap to produce, potent and persistent. DDT was used on a massive scale from the 1930s, with a peak of 72,000 tonnes used 1970. Then usage fell as the harmful environmental effects were realized. It was found worldwide in fish and birds and was even discovered in the snow in the Antarctic. It is only slightly soluble in water but is very soluble in the bloodstream. It affects the nervous and endocrine systems and causes the eggshells of birds to lack calcium causing them to be easily breakable. It is thought to be responsible for the decline of the numbers of birds of prey like ospreys and peregrine falcons in the 1950s - they are now recovering.

As well as increased concentration via the food chain, it is known to enter via permeable membranes, so fish get it through their gills. As it has low water solubility, it tends to stay at the water surface, so organisms that live there are most affected. DDT found in fish that formed part of the human food chain caused concern, but the levels found in the liver, kidney and brain tissues was less than 1ppm and in fat was 10 ppm which was below the level likely to cause harm. However, DDT was banned in Britain and America to stop the further build up of it in the food chain. The USA exploited this ban and sold DDT to developing countries, who could not afford the expensive replacement chemicals and who did not have such stringent regulations governing the use of pesticides. Some insects have developed a resistance to insecticides - e.g. the which carries malaria.

Organophosphates

Organophosphates, e.g. parathion, methyl parathion and about 40 other insecticides are available nationally. Parathion is highly toxic, methyl-parathion is less so and Malathion is generally considered safe as it has low toxicity and is rapidly broken down in the mammalian liver. This group works by preventing normal nerve transmission as cholinesterase is prevented from breaking down the transmitter substance acetylcholine, resulting in uncontrolled muscle movements.

Entry of a variety of pesticides into our water supplies causes concern to environmental groups, as in many cases the long term effects of these specific chemicals is not known.

Restrictions came into force in July 1985 and were so frequently broken that in 1987, formal proceedings were taken against the British government. Britain is still the only European state to use Aldrin and organochlorines, although it was supposed to stop in 1993. East Anglia has the worst record for pesticide contamination of drinking water. Of the 350 pesticides used in Britain, only 50 can be analyzed, which is worrying for the global community.

Burial

Burial is the technique used by Jews, Muslims, Christians and other religions with Abrahamic influence, to dispose off the corpse of dead humans and animals. This process leads to regular soil erosion due to loosening of soil. Also, the decomposing fluids act as poisonous herbicides, pesticides and may even lead to epidemics in surrounding areas. It leads to soil pollution, soil erosion and even water pollution.

Increased Waste Disposal

In Scotland in 1993, 14 million tons of waste was produced. 100,000 tons was special waste and 260,000 tons was controlled waste from other parts of Britain and abroad. 45% of the special waste was in liquid form and 18% was asbestos - radioactive waste was not included. Of the controlled waste, 48% came from the demolition of buildings, 22% from industry, 17% from households and 13% from business - only 3% were recycled. 90% of controlled waste was buried in landfill sites and produced 2 million tons of methane gas. 1.5% was burned in incinerators and 1.5% were exported to be disposed of or recycled. There are 748 disposal sites in Scotland.

Landfills produce leachate, which has to be recycled to keep favourable conditions for microbial activity, methane gas and some carbon dioxide.

There are very few vacant or derelict land sites in the north east of Scotland, as there are few traditional heavy industries or coal/mineral extraction sites. However some areas are contaminated by aromatic hydrocarbons (500 cubic meters).

The Urban Waste Water Treatment Directive allows sewage sludge to be sprayed onto land and the volume is expected to double to 185,000 tons of dry solids in 2005. This has good agricultural properties due to the high nitrogen and phosphate content. In 1990/1991, 13% wet weight was sprayed onto 0.13% of the land , however this is expected to rise 15 fold by 2005. There is a need to control this so that pathogenic microorganisms do not get into water courses and to ensure that there is no accumulation of heavy metals in the top soil.

3

ORE

An ore is a type of rock that contains minerals such as gemstones and metals that can be extracted through mining and refined for use. Samples of ore in the form of exceptionally beautiful crystals, exotic layering visible when sectioned or polished or metallic presentations such as large nuggets or crystalline formations of metals such as gold or copper may command a value far beyond their value as mere ore or raw metal for subsequent reduction to utilitarian purposes.

The grade or concentration of an ore mineral, or metal, as well as its form of occurrence, will directly affect the costs associated with mining the ore. The cost of extraction must thus be weighted against the contained metal value of the rock to determine what ore can be profitably extracted and what ore is of too low a grade to be worth mining. Metal ores are generally oxides, sulfides, silicates, or "native" metals (such as native copper) that are not commonly concentrated in the Earth's crust or "noble" metals (not usually forming compounds) such as gold. The ores must be processed to extract the metals of interest from the waste rock and from the ore minerals. Ore bodies are formed by a variety of geological processes. The process of ore formation is called ore genesis.

Ore Deposits

An ore deposit is an accumulation of ore. This is distinct from a mineral resource as defined by the mineral resource classification criteria. An ore deposit is one occurrence of the particular ore type. Most ore deposits are named according to either their location (for example the Witswatersrand, South Africa), or after a discoverer (eg; the kambalda nickel shoots are named after drillers), or after some whimsy, an historical figure, a prominent person,_something from mythology (phoenix, kraken, etc) or the code name of the resource company which found it (eg; MKD-5 is the in-house name for the Mount Keith nickel.

Classification of Ore Deposits

Ore deposits are classified according to various criteria developed via the study of economic geology, or ore genesis. The classifications below are typical.

Hydrothermal Epigenetic Deposits

- Mesothermal lode gold deposits, typified by the Golden Mile, Kalgoorlie.
- Archaean conglomerate hosted gold-uranium deposits, typified by Elliot Lake, Canada and Witwatersrand, South Africa.

Carlin type gold deposits, including:

- Dolomite-hosted jasperoid replacement subtype.
- Epithermal stockwork vein deposits.

Granite Related Hydrothermal

- IOCG or iron-oxide copper-gold, typified by the supergiant Olympic Dam Cu-Au-U deposit.

- Porphyry copper +/- gold +/- molybdenum +/- silver deposits.
- Intrusive-related copper-gold +/- (tin-tungsten), typified by the Tombstone, Arizona deposits.
- Hydromagmatic magnetite iron ore deposits and skarns.
- Skarn ore deposits of copper, lead, zinc, tungsten, etcetera.

Nickel-cobalt-platinum Deposits

- Magmatic nickel-copper-iron-PGE deposits including
- Cumulate vanadiferous or platinum-bearing magnetite or chromite.
- Cumulate hard-rock titanium (ilmenite) deposits.
- Komatiite hosted Ni-Cu-PGE deposits.
- Subvolcanic feeder subtype, typified by Noril'sk-Talnakh and the Thompson Belt, Canada.
- Intrusive-related Ni-Cu-PGE, typified by Voisey's Bay, Canada and Jinchuan, China.
- Lateritic nickel ore deposits, examples include Goro and Acoje, (Philippines) and Ravensthorpe, Western Australia.

Volcanic-related Deposits

Volcanic hosted massive sulfide (VHMS) Cu-Pb-Zn including:

- Examples include Teutonic Bore and Golden Grove, Western Australia.
- Besshi type.
- Kuroko type.

Metamorphically Reworked Deposits

- Podiform serpentinite-hosted paramagmatic iron oxide-chromite deposits, typified by Savage River, Tasmania iron ore, Coobina chromite deposit.

- Broken Hill Type Pb-Zn-Ag, considered to be a class of reworked SEDEX deposits

Carbonatite-alkaline Igneous Related

- Phosphorus-tantalite-vermiculite (Phalaborwa South Africa)
- Rare earth elements - Mount Weld, Australia and Bayan Obo, Mongolia.
- Diatreme hosted diamond in kimberlite, lamproite or lamprophyre

Sedimentary Deposits

Close-up of Banded Iron Formation specimen from Upper Michigan. Scale bar is 5.0 mm.

- Banded iron formation iron ore deposits, including:
  - Channel-iron deposits or pisolite type iron ore.
- Heavy mineral sands ore deposits and other sand dune hosted deposits.
- Alluvial gold, diamond, tin, platinum or black sand deposits.
- Alluvial oxide zinc deposit type: sole example Skorpion Zinc.

Sedimentary Hydrothermal Deposits

- SEDEX.
  - Lead-zinc-silver, typified by Red Dog, McArthur River, Mt Isa, etc.
  - Stratiform arkose-hosted and shale-hosted copper, typified by the Zambian copperbelt.
  - Stratiform tungsten, typified by the Erzgebirge deposits, Czechoslovakia.
  - Exhalative spilite-chert hosted gold deposits.
- Mississippi valley type (MVT) zinc-lead deposits.

- Hematite iron ore deposits of altered banded iron formation.

Astrobleme-related Ores

- Sudbury Basin nickel and copper, Ontario, Canada.

Extraction

The basic extraction of ore deposits follows the steps below:

- Prospecting or Exploration to find and then define the extent and value of ore where it is located ("ore body").
- Conduct resource estimation to mathematically estimate the size and grade of the deposit.
- Conduct a pre-feasibility study to determine the theoretical economics of the ore deposit. This identifies, early on, whether further investment in estimation and engineering studies is warranted and identifies key risks and areas for further work.
- Conduct a feasibility study to evaluate the financial viability, technical and financial risks and robustness of the project and make a decision as whether to develop or walk away from a proposed mine project. This includes mine planning to evaluate the economically recoverable portion of the deposit, the metallurgy and ore recoverability, marketability and payability of the ore concentrates, engineering, milling and infrastructure costs, finance and equity requirements and a cradle to grave analysis of the possible mine, from the initial excavation all the way through to reclamation.
- Development to create access to an ore body and building of mine plant and equipment.
- The operation of the mine in an active sense.
- Reclamation to make land where a mine had been suitable for future use.

Trade

Ores (metals) are traded internationally and comprise a sizeable portion of international trade in raw materials both in value and volume. This is because the worldwide distribution of ores is unequal and dislocated from locations of peak demand and from smelting infrastructure.

Most base metals (copper, lead, zinc, nickel) are traded internationally on the London Metal Exchange, with smaller stockpiles and metals exchanges monitored by the Comex and Nymex exchanges in the United States and the Shanghai Futures Exchange in China.

Iron ore is traded between customer and producer, though various benchmark prices are set yearly between the major mining conglomerates and the major consumers, and this sets the stage for smaller participants.

Other, lesser, commodities do not have international clearing houses and benchmark prices, with most prices negotiated between suppliers and customers one-on-one. This generally makes determining the price of ores of this nature opaque and difficult. Such metals include lithium, niobium-tantalum, bismuth, antimony and rare earths. Most of these commodities are also dominated by one or two major suppliers with >60% of the world's reserves. The London Metal Exchange aims to add uranium to its list of metals on warrant.

The World Bank reports that China was the top importer of ores and metals in 2005 followed by the USA and Japan.

Important Ore Minerals

- Acanthite: Ag_2S for production of silver.
- Barite: $BaSO_4$.
- Bauxite Al_2O_3 for production of aluminium.
- Beryl: $Be_3Al_2(SiO_3)_6$

- Bornite: Cu_5FeS_4
- Cassiterite: SnO_2
- Chalcocite: Cu_2S for production of copper
- Chalcopyrite: $CuFeS_2$
- Chromite: $(Fe, Mg)Cr_2O_4$ for production of chromium
- Cinnabar: HgS for production of mercury.
- Cobaltite: (Co, Fe)AsS
- Columbite-Tantalite or Coltan: $(Fe, Mn)(Nb, Ta)_2O_6$
- Galena: PbS
- Gold: Au, typically associated with quartz or as placer deposits.
- Hematite: Fe_2O_3
- Ilmenite: $FeTiO_3$
- Magnetite: Fe_3O_4
- Molybdenite: MoS_2
- Pentlandite: $(Fe, Ni)_9S_8$
- Pyrolusite:MnO_2
- Scheelite: $CaWO_4$
- Sphalerite: ZnS
- Uraninite (pitchblende): UO_2 for production of metallic uranium
- Wolframite: $(Fe, Mn)WO_4$

MINERAL RESOURCE CLASSIFICATION

Mineral resource classification is the systematic organization of information on ores and other mineral deposits which contain economic value. The process guides governmental and industrial planning on how to manage the resources.

Not all mineralization meets these criteria. The specific categories of mineralization in an economic sense are:

- *mineral occurrences* or prospects which are of geological interest but may not be of economic interest.
- *mineral resources,* include those which are potentially economically and technically feasible, and those which are not ore reserves, must be economically and technically feasible to extract.
- *Mineral reserves of ore reserves* that are valuable and economically and technically feasible to extract.

The common terminology for mining, "ore deposit", by definition must have an 'ore reserve', and may or may not have additional 'resources'.

Classification, because it is an economic function, is governed by statutes, regulations and industry best practice norms. There are several classification schemes worldwide, however the Canadian CIM classification (see NI 43-101) and the Australasian Joint Ore Reserves Committee Code (JORC Code) are the general standards.

Mineral Occurrences, Prospects

These classifications of mineral occurrences are generally the least important and least economic. They included are all known occurrences of minerals of economic interest, including obviously uneconomic outcrops and manifestations. However, these are often mentioned in a company prospectus because of "proximity"; a concept that something valuable may be found near these occurrences because it has been in the past due to a similar geological environment. Often, such occurrences of mineralisation are the peripheral manifestations of nearby ore deposits. "Ore deposit" is a term applied specifically to those economic mineral occurrences which could be mined at a profit after consideration of all factors impacting a mining operation.

Mineral Resources

Mineral resources are those economic mineral concentrations which have undergone enough scrutiny to quantify their contained metal to a certain degree. None of these resources are ore, because the economics of the mineral deposit may not have been fully evaluated.

Indicated resources are simply economic mineral occurrences which have been sampled (usually by drilling) to a point at which an estimate of their contained metal and grade has been made. Generally this is very approximate and subject to sampling errors and uncertainties.

Measured resources are indicated resources which have undergone enough further sampling that a 'competent person' (which is defined by the norms of the relevant mining code; usually a geologist) has declared them to be an acceptable estimate of the grade, tonnage and occurrence of the mineral occurrence.

Resources may also be portions of a mineral occurrence which are attached to reserves, but are:

- not sufficiently drilled out to qualify as Reserve status;
- too deep to economically extract;
- too deep to technically extract;
- too low of grade to economically or technically extract;
- contaminated, or refractory in nature;
- have not yet met all of the criteria for Reserve status.

Mineral Reserves

Mineral reserves are the resources which are known to be economically feasible for extraction. Reserves are either 'Probable Reserves or Proven Reserves, in a similar manner to resources, above. Generally the conversion of resources into reserves requires; knowledge of the geology of the deposit sufficient that it is predictable and verifiable consideration of metallurgy, including plans for extraction, mineral processing calculation and design of open pit or underground mine plans based on ore models quantification of geotechnical risk; basically, managing the geological faults, joints and fractures in the ground so the mine does not collapse consideration of technical risk; essentially, statistical and variography to ensure the ore is sampled properly scrutiny of the assay data to ensure the accuracy of the information supplied by the laboratory.

This is required because ore reserves are bankable. Essentially, once a deposit is brought up to reserve status, it is an economic entity and an asset upon which loans and equity can be drawn - generally in order to pay for its extraction (hopefully, at a profit).

MINERAL EXPLORATION

Mineral exploration is the process undertaken by companies, partnerships or corporations in the endeavour of finding ore (commercially viable concentrations of minerals) to mine. Mineral exploration is a much more intensive, organised and professional form of mineral prospecting and, though it frequently uses the services of prospecting, the process of mineral exploration on the whole is much more involved.

Stages of Mineral Exploration

Area Selection

Area selection is a crucial step in professional mineral exploration. Selection of the best, most prospective, area in a mineral field, geological region or terrain will assist in making it not only possible to find ore deposits, but to find them easily, cheaply and quickly.

Area selection is based on applying the theories behind ore genesis, the knowledge of known ore occurrences and the method of their formation, to known geological regions via the study of geological maps, to determine potential areas where the particular class of ore deposit being sought may exist.

This process applies the disciplines of basin modeling, structural geology, geochronology, petrology and a host of geophysical and geochemical disciplines to make predictions and draw parallels between the known ore deposits and their physical form and the unknown potential of finding a 'lookalike' within the area selected.

Area selection is also influenced by the commodity being sought; exploring for gold occurs in a different manner and within different rocks and areas to exploration for oil or natural gas or iron ore. Areas which are prospective for gold may not be prospective for other metals and commodities.

Often a company or consortium wishing to enter mineral exploration may conduct market research to determine, if a resource in a particular commodity is found, whether or not the resource will be worth mining based on projected commodity prices and demand growth.

Area selection may also be influenced by previous finds, a practice affectionately named nearology, and may also be determined in part by financial and taxation incentives and tariff systems of individual nations. The role of infrastructure may also be crucial in area selection, because the ore must be brought to market and infrastructure costs may render isolated ore uneconomic.

The ultimate result of an area selection process is the pegging or notification of exploration licenses, known as tenements.

Target Generation

The target generation phase involves investigations of the geology via mapping, geophysics and conducting geochemical or intensive geophysical testing of the surface and subsurface geology. In some cases, for instance in areas covered by soil, alluvium and platform cover, drilling may be performed directly as a mechanism for generating targets.

Geophysical Methods

Geophysical instruments play a large role in gathering geological data which is used in mineral exploration.

Instruments are used in geophysical surveys to check for variations in gravity, magnetism, electromagnetism (conductivity and resistivity of rocks) and a number of different other variables in a certain area. The most effective and widespread method of gathering geophysical data is via flying airborne geophysics.

Geiger counters and scintillometers are used to determine the amount of radioactivity. This is particularly applicable to searching for uranium ore deposits but can also be of use in detecting radiometric anomalies associated with metasomatism.

Airborne magnetometers are used to search for magnetic anomalies in the Earth's magnetic field. The anomalies are an indication of concentrations of magnetic minerals such as magnetite, pyrrhotite and ilmenite in the Earth's crust. It is often the case that such magnetic anomalies are caused by mineralization events and associated metals.

Ground-based geophysical prospecting in the target selection stage is more limited, due to the time and cost. The most widespread use of ground-based geophysics is electromagnetic geophysics which detects conductive minerals such as sulfide minerals within more resistive host rocks.

Ultraviolet lamps may cause certain minerals to fluoresce, and is a key tool in prospecting for tungsten mineralisation.

Remote Sensing

Aerial photography is an important tool in assessing mineral exploration tenements, as it gives the explorer orientation information - location of tracks, roads, fences, habitation, as well as ability to at least qualitatively map outcrops and regolith systematics and vegetation cover across a region. Aerial photography was first used post World War II and was heavily adopted in the 1960's onwards.

Since the advent of cheap and declassified Landsat images in the late 1970's an early 1980's, mineral exploration has begun to use satellite imagery to map not only the visual light spectrum over mineral exploration tenements but spectra which are beyond the visible.

Satellite based spectroscopes allow the modern mineral explorationist, in regions devoid of cover and vegetation, to map minerals and alteration directly. Improvements in the resolution of modern commercially based satellites has also improved the utility of satellite imagery; for instance IKONIS satellite images can be generated with a 30cm pixel size.

Geochemical Methods

The primary role of geochemistry, here used to describe assaying or geological media, in mineral exploration is to find an area anomalous in the commodity sought, or in elements known to be associated with the type of mineralisation sought.

Regional geochemical exploration has traditionally involved use of stream sediments to target potentially mineralised catchments. Regional surveys may use low sampling densities such as one sample per 100 square kilometres. Follow-up geochemical surveys commonly use soils as the sampling media, possibly via the collection of a grid of samples over the tenement or areas which are amenable to soil geochemistry. Areas which are covered by transported soils, alluvium, colluvium or are disturbed too much by human activity (roads, rail, farmland), may need to be drilled to a shallow depth in order to sample undisturbed or unpolluted bedrock.

Once the geochemical analyses are returned, the data is investigated for anomalies (single or multiple elements) that may be related to the presence of mineralisation. The geochemical anomaly is often field checked against the outcropping geology and, in modern geochemistry, normalised against the regolith type and landform, to reduce the effects of weathering, transported materials and landforms.

Geochemical anomalies may be spurious or related to low-grade or sub-grade mineralisation. In order to determine if this is the case, geochemical anomalies must be drilled in order to test them for the existence of economic concentrations of mineralisation, or even to determine why they exist in the place they exist.

The presence of some chemical elements may indicate the presence of a certain mineral. Chemical analysis of rocks and plants may indicate the presence of an underground deposit. For instance elements like arsenic and antimony are associated with gold deposits and hence, are example pathfinder elements. Tree buds can be sampled for pathfinder elements in order to help locate deposits.

Resource Evaluation

Resource evaluation is undertaken to quantify the grade and tonnage of a mineral occurrence. This is achieved primarily by drilling to sample the prospective horizon, lode or strata where the minerals of interest occur.

The ultimate aim is to generate a density of drilling sufficient to satisfy the economic and statutory standards of an ore resource. Depending on the financial situation and size of the deposit and the structure of the company, the level of detail required to generate this resource and stage at which extraction can commence varies; for small partnerships and private non-corporate enterprises a very low level of detail is required whereas for corporations which require debt equity (loans) to build capital intensive extraction infrastructure, the rigor necessary in resource estimation is far greater. For large cash rich companies working on small ore bodies, they may work only to a level necessary to satisfy their internal risk assessments before extraction commences.

Resource estimation may require pattern drilling on a set grid, and in the case of sulfide minerals, will usually require some form of geophysics such as down-hole probing of drillholes, to geophysically delineate ore body continuity within the ground.

The aim of resource evaluation is to expand the known size of the deposit and mineralisation. A scoping study is often carried out on the ore deposit during this stage to determine if there may be enough ore at a sufficient grade to warrant extraction; if there is not further resource evaluation drilling may be necessary. In other cases, several smaller individually uneconomic deposits may be socialised into a 'mining camp' and extracted in tandem. Further exploration and testing of anomalies may be required to find or define these other satellite deposits.

Reserve Definition

Reserve definition is undertaken to convert a mineral resource into an ore reserve, which is an economic asset. The process is similar to resource evaluation, except more intensive and technical, aimed at statistically quantifying the grade continuity and mass of ore.

Reserve definition also takes into account the milling and extractability characteristics of the ore, and generates bulk samples for metallurgical testwork, involving crushability, floatability and other ore recovery parameters.

Reserve definition includes geotechnical assessment and engineering studies of the rocks within and surrounding the deposit to determine the potential instabilities of proposed open pit or underground mining methods. This process may involve drilling diamond core samples to derive structural information on weaknesses within the rock mass such as faults, foliations, joints and shearing.

At the end of this process, a feasibility study is published, and the ore deposit may be either deemed uneconomic or economic.

Extraction

The ultimate goal of mineral exploration is the extraction, beneficiation and profitable and beneficial sale of mineral commodities.

Extraction methods may vary considerably and it is the discipline of engineers trained in mining engineering to determine the most safe, cost effective and efficient method of mining the ore body.

Mineral exploration and development does not cease upon a decision to mine. Exploration of a brownfields nature is conducted to find near-mine repetitions, extensions and continuity of the existing ore body. In-mine exploration and grade control drilling is a major concern of operating mines and can be an effective tool in adding value to existing mineral operations.

Often the lessons learned from studying an exposed ore body, both empirically and scientifically, are invaluable to the exploration geologist and geophysicist, for they get to see the proof of their concepts and the errors of the assumptions they used in the search for the ore body. It is always the case that the exact nature of the ore body does not exactly match the models used to find it.

Greenfields vs Brownfields

Exploration is termed either Greenfields or Brownfields depending on the extent to which previous exploration has been conducted on the tenements in question. Greenfields alludes to unspoilt grass, and brownfields to that which has been trodden on repeatedly. While loosely defined, the general meaning of brownfields exploration is that which is conducted within geological terranes within close proximity to known ore deposits. Greenfields are the remainder.

Greenfields exploration is highly conceptual, relying on the predictive power of ore genesis models to search for mineralisation in unexplored virgin ground. This may be territory which has been drilled for other commodities, but with a new exploration concept is considered prospective for commodities not sought there before.

The success rate of exploration and the return on investment is low because exploration is an inherently risky business. Figures for success rates depend on the commodity in question but a good strike rate can be measured in the oil industry; the supergiant Prudhoe Bay oilfield was found on the 12th well drilled into the area. Within gold deposits a discovery hole may be one in one thousand and within some base metals commodities strike rates range from one in fifty to one in one hundred.

Greenfields exploration has a lower strike rate, because the geology is poorly understood at the conception of an exploration program but the rewards are greater because it is easier to find the biggest deposit in an area earlier, and it is only with more effort that the smaller satellite deposits are found. Brownfields exploration is less risky, as the geology is better understood and exploration methodology is well known, but since most large deposits are already found the rewards are incrementally less.

4

ORE GENESIS

The various theories of ore genesis explain how the various types of mineral deposits form within the Earth's crust. Ore genesis theories are very dependent on the mineral or commodity.

Ore genesis theories generally involve three components: source, transport or conduit, and trap. This also applies to the petroleum industry, which was first to use this methodology.

- Source is required because metal must come from somewhere, and be liberated by some process.
- Transport is required first to move the metal bearing fluids or solid minerals into the right position, and refers to the act of physically moving the metal, as well as chemical or physical phenomenon which encourage movement.
- Trapping is required to concentrate the metal via some physical, chemical or geological mechanism into a concentration which forms mineable ore.

The biggest deposits are formed when the source is large, the transport mechanism is efficient, and the trap is active and ready at the right time.

Ore Genesis Processes

Evans (1993) divides ore genesis into the following main categories based on physical process. These are internal processes, hydrothermal processes, metamorphic processes and surficial processes.

Internal Processes

These processes are integral physical phenomena and chemical reactions internal to magmas, generally in plutonic or volcanic rocks. These include:

- *Fractional crystallization*, either creating monomineralic cumulate ores or contributing to the enrichment of ore minerals and metals.
- *Liquation, or liquid immiscibility* between melts of differing composition, usually sulfide segregations of nickel-copper-platinoid sulfides and silicates.

Hydrothermal Processes

These processes are the physico-chemical phenomena and reactions caused by movement of hydrothermal waters within the crust, often as a consequence of magmatic intrusion or tectonic upheavals. The foundations of hydrothermal processes are the source-transport-trap mechanism.

Sources of hydrothermal solutions include seawater, formational brines (water trapped within sediments at deposition) and metamorphic fluids created by dehydration of hydrous minerals during metamorphism.

Metal sources may include a plethora of rocks. However most metals of economic importance are carried as trace elements within rock-forming minerals, and so may be liberated by hydrothermal processes. This happens because of:

- incompatibility of the metal with its host mineral, for example zinc in calcite, which favours aqueous fluids in contact with the host mineral under diagenesis;
- solubility of the host mineral within nascent hydrothermal solutions in the source rocks, for example mineral salts (halite), carbonates (cerussite), phosphates (monazite and thorianite) and sulfates (barite);
- elevated temperatures causing decomposition reactions of minerals.

Transport by hydrothermal solutions usually requires a salt or other soluble species which can form a metal-bearing complex. These metal-bearing complexes facilitate transport of metals within aqueous solutions, generally as hydroxides, but also by processes similar to chelation.

This process is especially well understood in gold metallogeny where various thiosulfate, chloride and other gold-carrying chemical complexes (notably tellurium-chloride/sulfate or antimony-chloride/sulfate). The majority of metal deposits formed by hydrothermal processes include sulfide minerals, indicating sulfur is an important metal-carrying complex.

Sulfide Deposition

Sulfide deposition within the trap zone occurs when metal-carrying sulfate, sulfide or other complexes become chemically unstable due to one or more of the following processes:

- falling temperature, which renders the complex unstable or metal insoluble;
- loss of pressure, which has the same effect;
- reaction with chemically reactive wall rocks, usually of reduced oxidation state, such as iron bearing rocks, mafic or ultramafic rocks or carbonate rocks;

- degassing of the hydrothermal fluid into a gas and water system, or boiling, which alters the metal carrying capacity of the solution and even destroys metal-carrying chemical complexes.

Metal can also become precipitated when temperature and pressure or oxidation state favour different ionic complexes in the water, for instance the change from sulfide to sulfate, oxygen fugacity, exchange of metals between sulfide and chloride complexes, etc.

Metamorphic Processes

Lateral Secretion

Ore deposits formed by lateral secretion are formed by metamorphic reactions during shearing, which liberate mineral constituents such as quartz, sulfides, gold, carbonates and oxides from deforming rocks and focus these constituents into zones of reduced pressure or dilation such as faults. This may occur without much hydrothermal fluid flow, and this is typical of podiform chromite deposits.

Metamorphic processes also control many physical processes which form the source of hydrothermal fluids, outlined above.

Surficial Processes

Surficial processes are the physical and chemical phenomena which cause concentration of ore material within the regolith, generally by the action of the environment. This includes placer deposits, laterite deposits and residual or eluvial deposits. The physical processes of ore deposit formation in the surficial realm include:

- erosion;
- deposition by sedimentary processes, including winnowing, density separation (e.g; gold placers);

- weathering via oxidation or chemical attack of a rock, either liberating rock fragments or creating chemically deposited clays, laterites or manto ore deposits.
- deposition in low-energy environments in beach environments.

Classification of Ore Deposits

Ore deposits are usually classified by ore formation processes and geological setting. For example, SEDEX deposits, literally meaning "sedimentary exhalative" are a class of ore deposit formed on the sea floor (sedimentary) by exhalation of brines into seawater (exhalative), causing chemical precipitation of ore minerals when the brine cools, mixes with sea water and loses its metal carrying capacity.

Ore deposits rarely fit snugly into the boxes in which geologists wish to place them. Many may be formed by one or more of the basic genesis processes above, creating ambiguous classifications and much argument and conjecture. Often ore deposits are classified after examples of their type, for instance Broken Hill Type lead-zinc-silver deposits or Carlin-type Gold deposits.

Classification of hydrothermal ore deposits is also achieved by classifying according to the temperature of formation, which roughly also correlates with particular mineralising fluids, mineral associations and structural styles. This scheme, proposed by Waldemar Lindgren (1933) classified hydrothermal deposits as hypothermal, mesothermal, epithermal and telethermal.

GENESIS OF COMMON ORES

This page has been organised by metal commodity; it is also possible to organise theories according to geological criteria of formation, as well as by metal association. Often ores of the same metal can be formed by multiple processes, and this is described by commodity.

Iron Ore

Iron ores are overwhelmingly derived from ancient sediments known as banded iron formations (BIFs). These sediments are composed of iron oxide minerals deposited on the sea floor. Particular environmental conditions are needed to transport enough iron in sea water to form these deposits, such as acidic and oxygen-poor atmospheres within the Proterozoic Era.

Often, more recent weathering during the Tertiary or Eocene is required to convert the usual magnetite minerals into more easily processed hematite. Some iron deposits within the Pilbara of West Australia are placer deposits, formed by accumulation of hematite gravels called pisolites which form channel-iron deposits. These are preferred because they are cheap to mine.

Lead Zinc Silver

Lead-zinc deposits are generally accompanied by silver, hosted within the lead sulfide mineral galena or within the zinc sulfide mineral sphalerite.

Lead and zinc deposits are formed by discharge of deep sedimentary brine onto the sea floor (termed sedimentary exhalative or SEDEX), or by replacement of limestone, in skarn deposits, some associated with submarine volcanoes (called volcanogenic massive sulfide ore deposits or VMS) or in the aureole of subvolcanic intrusions of granite. The vast majority of SEDEX lead and zinc deposits are Proterozoic in age, although there are significant Jurassic examples in Canada and Alaska.

The carbonate replacement type deposit is exemplified by the Mississippi valley type (MVT) ore deposits. MVT and similar styles occur by replacement and degradation of carbonate sequences by hydrocarbons, which are thought important for transporting lead.

Gold

Gold deposits are formed via a very wide variety of geological processes. Deposits are classified as primary, alluvial or placer deposits, or residual or laterite deposits. Often a deposit will contain a mixture of all three types of ore.

Plate tectonics is the underlying mechanism for generating gold deposits. The majority of primary gold deposits fall into two main categories: lode gold deposits or intrusion-related deposits.

Lode gold deposits are generally high-grade, thin, vein and fault hosted. They are comprised primarily of quartz veins also known as lodes or reefs, which contain either native gold or gold sulfides and tellurides. Lode gold deposits are usually hosted in basalt or in sediments known as turbidite, although when in faults, they may occupy intrusive igneous rocks such as granite.

Lode-gold deposits are intimately associated with orogeny and other plate collision events within geologic history. Most lode gold deposits sourced from metamorphic rocks because it is thought that the majority are formed by dehydration of basalt during metamorphism. The gold is transported up faults by hydrothermal waters and deposited when the water cools too much to retain gold in solution.

Intrusive related gold is generally hosted in granites, porphyry or rarely dikes. Intrusive related gold usually also contains copper, and is often associated with tin and tungsten, and rarely molybdenum, antimony and uranium. Intrusive-related gold deposits rely on gold existing in the fluids associated with the magma and the inevitable discharge of these hydrothermal fluids into the wall-rocks. Skarn deposits are another manifestation of intrusive-related deposits.

Placer deposits are sourced from pre-existing gold deposits and are secondary deposits. Placer deposits are formed by alluvial processes within rivers, streams and on beaches. Placer gold deposits form via gravity, with the density of gold causing it to sink into trap sites within the river bed, or where water velocity drops, such as bends in rivers and behind boulders. Often placer deposits are found within sedimentary rocks and can be billions of years old, for instance the Witwatersrand deposits in South Africa. Sedimentary placer deposits are known as 'leads' or 'deep leads'.

Placer deposits are often worked by fossicking, and panning for gold is a popular pastime.

Laterite gold deposits are formed from pre-existing gold deposits (including some placer deposits) during prolonged weathering of the bedrock. Gold is deposited within iron oxides in the weathered rock or regolith, and may be further enriched by reworking by erosion. Some laterite deposits are formed by wind erosion of the bedrock leaving a residuum of native gold metal at surface.

Platinum

Platinum and palladium are precious metals generally found in ultramafic rocks. The source of platinum and palladium deposits is ultramafic rocks which have enough sulfur to form a sulfide mineral while the magma is still liquid. This sulfide mineral (usually pentlandite, pyrite, chalcopyrite or pyrrhotite) gains platinum by mixing with the bulk of the magma because platinum is chalcophile and is concentrated in sulfides. Alternatively, platinum occurs in association with chromite either within the chromite mineral itself or within sulfides associated with it.

Sulfide phases only form in ultramafic magmas when the magma reaches' sulfur saturation. This is generally thought to be nearly impossible by pure fractional crystallisation, so other processes are usually required in ore genesis models to explain sulfur saturation. These include contamination of the magma with crustal material, especially sulfur-rich wall-rocks or sediments; magma mixing; volatile gain or loss.

Often platinum is associated with nickel, copper, chromium, and cobalt deposits.

Nickel

Nickel deposits are generally found in two forms, either as sulfide or laterite.

Sulfide type nickel deposits are formed in essentially the same manner as platinum deposits. Nickel is a chalcophile element which prefers sulfides, so an ultramafic or mafic rock which has a sulfide phase in the magma may form nickel sulfides. The best nickel deposits are formed where sulfide accumulates in the base of lava tubes or volcanic flows — especially komatiite lavas.

Komatiitic nickel-copper sulfide deposits are considered to be formed by a mixture of sulfide segregation, immiscibility, and thermal erosion of sulfidic sediments. The sediments are considered to be necessary to promote sulfur saturation.

Some subvolcanic sills in the Thompson Belt of Canada host nickel sulfide deposits formed by deposition of sulfides near the feeder vent. Sulfide was accumulated near the vent due to the loss of magma velocity at the vent interface. The massive Voisey's Bay nickel deposit is considered to have formed via a similar process.

The process of forming nickel laterite deposits is essentially similar to the formation of gold laterite deposits, except that ultramafic or mafic rocks are required. Generally nickel laterites require very large olivine-bearing ultramafic intrusions. Minerals formed in laterite nickel deposits include gibbsite.

Copper

Copper is found in association with many other metals and deposit styles. Commonly, copper is either formed within sedimentary rocks, or associated with igneous rocks.

The world's major copper deposits are formed within the granitic porphyry copper style. Copper is enriched by processes during crystallisation of the granite and forms as chalcopyrite — a sulfide mineral, which is carried up with the granite.

Sometimes granites erupt to suface as volcanoes, and copper mineralisation forms during this phase when the granite and volcanic rocks cool via hydrothermal circulation.

Sedimentary copper forms within ocean basins in sedimentary rocks. Generally this forms by brine from deeply buried sediments discharging into the deep sea, and precipitating copper and often lead and zinc sulfides directly onto the sea floor. This is then buried by further sediment.

Often copper is associated with gold, lead, zinc and nickel deposits.

Uranium

Uranium deposits are usually sourced from radioactive granites, where certain minerals such as monazite are leached during hydrothermal activity or during circulation of groundwater. The uranium is brought into solution by acidic conditions and is deposited when this acidity is neutralised. Generally this occurs in certain carbon-bearing sediments, within an unconformity in sedimentary strata. The majority of the world's nuclear power is sourced from uranium in such deposits.

Uranium is also found in nearly all coal at several parts per million, and in all granites. Radon is a common problem during mining of uranium as it is a radioactive gas.

Uranium is also found associated with certain igenous rocks, such as granite and porphyry. The Olympic Dam deposit in Australia is an example of this type of uranium deposit. It contains 70% of Australia's share of 40% of the known global low-cost recoverable uranium inventory.

Titanium or Zirconium

Mineral sands are the predominant type of titanium, zirconium and thorium deposit. They are formed by accumulation of such heavy minerals within beach systems, and are a type of placer deposits. The minerals which contain titanium are ilmenite, rutile and leucoxene, zirconium is contained within zircon, and thorium is generally contained within monazite. These minerals are sourced from primarily granite bedrock by erosion and transported to the sea by rivers where they accumulate within beach sands. Rarely, but importantly, gold, tin and platinum deposits can form in beach placer deposits.

Tin, Tungsten and Molybdenum

These three metals generally form in a certain type of granite, via a similar mechanism to intrusive-related gold and copper. They are considered together because the process of forming these deposits is essentially the same. Skarn type mineralisation related to these granites is a very important type of tin, tungsten and molybdenum deposit. Skarn deposits form by reaction of mineralised fluids from the granite reacting with wall rocks such as limestone. Skarn mineralisation is also important in lead, zinc, copper, gold and occasionally uranium mineralisation.

Greisen granite is another related tin-molybdenum and topaz mineralisation style.

Rare Earth Elements, Niobium, Tantalum, Lithium

The overwhelming majority of rare earth elements, tantalum and lithium are found within pegmatite. Ore genesis theories for these ores are wide and varied, but most involve metamorphism and igneous activity. Lithium is present as spodumene or lepidolite within pegmatite.

Carbonatite intrusions are an important source of these elements. Ore minerals are essentially part of the unusual mineralogy of carbonatite.

Phosphate

Phosphate is used in fertilisers. Immense quantities of phosphate rock or phosphorite occur in sedimentary shelf deposits, ranging Phosphate deposits are thought to be sourced from the skeletons of dead sea creatures which accumulated on the seafloor. Similar to iron ore deposits and oil, particular conditions in the ocean and environment are thought to have contributed to these deposits within the geological past.

Phosphate deposits are also formed from alkaline igneous rocks such as nepheline syenites, carbonatites and associated rock types. The phosphate is, in this case, contained within magmatic apatite, monazite or other rare-earth phosphates.

CONVECTION

Convection in the most general terms refers to the movement of molecules within fluids liquids, gases and rheids). Convection is one of the major modes of heat transfer and mass transfer. In fluids, convective heat and mass transfer take place through both diffusion – the random Brownian motion of individual particles in the fluid – and by advection, in which matter or heat is transported by the larger-scale motion of currents in the fluid. In the context of heat and mass transfer, the term "convection" is used to refer to the sum of advective and diffusive transfer.

Convection Heat Transfer

A common use of the term convection leaves out the word "heat" but nevertheless refers to heat convection: that is, the case in which heat is the entity of interest being advected (carried), and diffused (dispersed).

In one of two major types of heat convection, the heat is carried passively by a fluid motion which would occur anyway without the heating process. This heat transfer process is often termed "forced convection" or occasionally "heat advection."

In the other major type of heat convection, heating itself may cause the fluid motion (via expansion and buoyancy force), while at the same time also causing heat to be transported by this bulk motion of the fluid. This process is called natural convection, or "free convection". In the latter case, the problem of heat transport (and related transport of other substances in the fluid due to it) is generally more complicated. Both forced and natural types of heat convection may occur together.

Natural Convective Heat Transfer

Papers lifted on rising convective air current from warm radiatorMain article: Convective heat transfer.

When heat is transferred by the circulation of fluids due to buoyancy from the density changes induced by heating itself, then the process is known as free or natural convective heat transfer.

Familiar examples are the upward flow of air due to a fire or hot object and the circulation of water in a pot that is heated from below.

For a visual experience of natural convection, a glass that is full of hot water filled with red food dye may be placed inside a fish tank with cold, clear water. The convection currents of the red liquid will be seen to rise and also fall, then eventually settle, illustrating the process as heat gradients are dissipated.

Forced Convection

Natural heat convection (also called free convection) is distinguished from various types of forced heat convection, which refer to heat advection by a fluid which is not due to the natural forces of buoyancy induced by heating. In forced heat convection, transfer of heat is due to movement in the fluid which results from many other forces, such as (for example) a fan or pump. A convection oven thus works by forced convection, as a fan which rapidly circulates hot air forces heat into food faster than would naturally happen due to simple heating without the fan. Aerodynamic heating is a form of forced convection. Common fluid heat-radiator systems, and also heating and cooling of parts of the body by blood circulation, are other familiar examples of forced convection.

Flames and Convection

In a zero-gravity environment, there can be no buoyancy forces, and thus no natural (free) convection possible, so flames in many circumstances without gravity, smother in their own waste gases. However, flames may be maintained with any type of forced convection (breeze); or (in high oxygen environments in "still" gas environments) entirely from the minimal forced convection that occurs as heat-induced expansion (not buoyancy) of gases allows for ventilation of the flame, as waste gases move outward and cool, and fresh high-oxygen gas moves in to take up the low pressure zones created when flame-exhaust water condenses

Buoyancy Induced Convection not due to Heat

The general term for this is gravitational convection. Gravitational heat convection is the same as free convection. However, differential buoyancy forces which cause convection in gravity fields may result from sources of density variations in fluids other than those produced by heat, such as variable composition. For example, diffusion of a source of dry salt downward into wet soil assisted by the mechanism of the fact that saline is heavier than fresh water, is a type of gravitational convection Variable salinity in water and variable water content in air masses, are frequent causes of convection in the oceans and atmosphere, which do not involve heat, or else involve additional compositional density factors other than the density changes from thermal expansion (see thermohaline circulation). Similarly, variable composition within the Earth's interior which has not yet achieved maximal stability and minimal energy (in other words, with densest parts deepest) continues to cause a fraction of the convection of fluid rock and molten metal within the Earth's interior.

Oceanic Convection

Solar radiation also affects the oceans. Warm water from the Equator tends to circulate toward the poles, while cold polar water heads towards the Equator. Oceanic convection is also frequently driven by density differences due to varying salinity, known as thermohaline convection, and is of crucial importance in the global thermohaline circulation. In this case it is quite possible for relatively warm, saline water to sink, and colder, fresher water to rise, reversing the normal transport of heat.

Mantle Convection

Convection within Earth's mantle is the driving force for plate tectonics. There are actually two convection currents occurring within the Earth. The outer core experiences convective turnover of fluid metals (primarily iron and nickel). This convection is thought to be the driving force for the Earth's magnetic field through a still poorly understood mechanism.

As heat from the inner and outer core heat the lower portion of the mantle, a second set of convective currents form. This mantle convection is extremely slow, as the mantle is a thick semi-solid with the consistency of a very thick paste. This slow convection can take millions of years to complete one cycle.

Neutrino flux measurements from the Earth's core (see kamLAND) show the source of about two-thirds of the heat in the inner core is the radioactive decay of 40K, uranium and thorium. This has allowed plate tectonics on Earth to continue far longer than it would have if it were simply driven by heat left over from Earth's formation; or with heat produced from gravitational potential energy, as a result of physical rearrangement of denser portions of the Earth's interior toward the center of the planet (i.e., a type of prolonged falling and settling).

Vibration Convection in Gravity Fields

Vibration-induced convection occurs in powders and granulated materials in containers subject to vibration, in a gravity field. When the container accelerates upward, the bottom of the container pushes the entire contents upward. In contrast, when the container accelerates downward, the sides of the container push the adjacent material downward by friction, but the material more remote from the sides is less affected. The net result is a slow circulation of particles downward at the sides, and upward in the middle.

If the container contains particles of different sizes, the downward-moving region at the sides is often narrower than the larger particles. Thus, larger particles tend to become sorted to the top of such a mixture.

Scale and Rate of Convection

Convection may happen in fluids at all scales larger than a few atoms. Convection occurs on a large scale in atmospheres, oceans, and planetary mantles. Current movement during convection may be invisibly slow, or it may be obvious and rapid, as in a hurricane. On astronomical scales, convection of gas and dust is thought to occur in the accretion disks of black holes, at speeds which may closely approach that of light.

Pattern Formation

A fluid under Rayleigh-Bénard convection: the left picture represents the thermal field and the right picture its two-dimensional Fourier transform. Convection, especially Rayleigh-Bénard convection, where the convecting fluid is contained by two rigid horizontal plates, is a convenient example of a pattern forming system.

When heat is fed into the system from one direction (usually below), at small values it merely diffuses (conducts) from below upward, without causing fluid flow. As the heat flow is increased, above a critical value of the Rayleigh number, the system undergoes a bifurcation from the stable conducting state to the convecting state, where bulk motion of the fluid due to heat begins. If fluid parameters other than density do not depend significantly on temperature, the flow profile is symmetric, with the same volume of fluid rising as falling. This is known as Boussinesq convection.

As the temperature difference between the top and bottom of the fluid becomes higher, significant differences in fluid parameters other than density may develop in the fluid due to temperature. An example of such a parameter is viscosity, which may begin to significantly vary horizontally across layers of fluid. This breaks the symmetry of the system, and generally changes the pattern of up- and down-moving fluid from stripes to hexagons, as seen at right. Such hexagons are one example of a convection cell.

As the Rayleigh number is increased even further above the value where convection cells first appear, the system may undergo other bifurcations, and other more complex patterns, such as spirals, may begin to appear.

Atmospheric Convection

Atmospheric convection is the result of a parcel-environment instability, or temperature difference, layer in the atmosphere. It is often responsible for adverse weather throughout the world.

Overview

There are a few general archetypes of atmospheric instability that correspond to convection and lack thereof. Steeper and/or positive lapse rates (environmental air cools quickly with height) suggests atmospheric convection is more likely, while weaker and/or negative environmental lapse rates would suggest it is less likely. This is due to the fact that any displaced air parcels will become more (less) buoyant, given their sign of adiabatic temperature change, in the steep (weak) lapse rate environments.

Convection begins at the Level of Free Convection (LFC), where it begins its ascent through the Free Convective Layer (FCL), and then stops at the equilibrium level. The rising parcel, if having enough momentum, will continue to rise to the Maximum Parcel Level (MPL) until negative buoyancy decelerates the parcel to a stop.

As long as a parcel is convecting, it theoretically will be accelerating. The exception to this is if drag produced by the updraft creates an equal, albeit opposite force to counter that from the buoyancy This could be thought of as similar to the terminal velocity of a falling object. This force from buoyancy can be measured by Convective Available Potential Energy (CAPE), or the joules of energy available per kilogram of potentially buoyant air. A theoretical updraft velocity can be derived from this value via substitution into the kinetic energy equation. Although this value will be an underestimation given the aforementioned drag or entrainment effects holding back further acceleration at some point. See the CAPE, buoyancy, and parcel links for a more in depth mathematical explanation of these processes.

Initiation

The initiation of the convection requires the onset of certain parameters of the atmospheric profile. The driving force behind convection is instability, which requires, as said before, a difference in temperature between some parcel of air and the environmental air surrounding it. Certain atmospheric conditions and setups are known to be conducive to this temperature difference. The idea behind convection, especially that which leads to vertically growing cumulus towers (I.E. cumulus congestus), and cumuloform precipitation (Deep Moist Convection (DMC)), is that latent heat release supplies the necessary energy to keep the rising air buoyant. The lapse rate of rising air, before it can reach the condensation level, is such that it is almost always cooler than the environment. The latent heat release from condensation is the determinate between significant convection and almost no convection at all. The fact that air is generally cooler during winter months, and therefore can not hold as much water vapor and associated latent heat, is why significant convection (thunderstorms) are infrequent in cooler areas during that period. Thundersnow is one situation where forcing mechanisms provide support for very steep environmental lapse rates, which as mentioned before is an archetype for favored convection. The small amount of latent heat released from air rising and condensing moisture in a thundersnow also serves to increase this convective potential, although minimally.

Boundaries and Forcing

Despite the fact that there might be a layer in the atmosphere that has positive values of CAPE, if the parcel does not reach or begin rising to that level, the most significant convection that occurs in the FCL will not be realized. This can occur for numerous reasons. Primarily, it is the result of a cap, or convective inhibition (CIN/CINH). Processes that can erode this inhibition are heating of the earth's surface and forcing. Such forcing mechanisms encourage upward vertical velocity, characterized by a speed that is relatively low to what you find in a thunderstorm updraft. Because of this, it is not the actual air being pushed to its LFC that "breaks through" the inhibition, but rather the forcing cools the inhibition adiabatically. This would counter, or "erode" the increase of temperature with height that is present during a capping inversion.

Forcing mechanisms that can lead to the eroding of inhibition are ones that create some sort of evacuation of mass in the upper parts of the atmosphere, or a surplus of mass in the low levels of the atmosphere, which would lead to upper level divergence or lower level convergence, respectively. Upward vertical motion will often follow. Specifically, a cold front, sea/lake breeze, outflow boundary, or forcing through vorticity dynamics (differential positive vorticity advection) of the atmosphere such as with troughs, both shortwave and longwave. Jet streak dynamics through the imbalance of Coriolis and pressure gradient forces, causing subgeostrophic and supergeostrophic flows, can also create upward vertical velocities.There are numerous other atmospheric setups in which upward vertical velocities can be created.

Concerns Regarding Severe Deep Moist Convection

Buoyancy is key to thunderstorm growth and is necessary for any of the severe threats within a thunderstorm. It should be noted that there are other processes, not necessarily thermodynamic, that can increase updraft strength. These include updraft rotation, low level convergence, and evacuation of mass out of the top of the updraft via strong upper level winds and the jet stream.

Hail

An updraft that realizes a larger CAPE profile will theoretically have an updraft with a higher velocity (which will be referred to as a "stronger updraft" from this point on). A stronger updraft will increase the residence time of any condensation nuclei and their continued growth into hail stones (accretion). If this process occurs in the favored hail growth zone, which is above the freezing level/around the -20° C level and can be achieved by a stronger updraft, then the larger hail potential increases. Thus, a stronger updraft can lead to larger hail.

The amount of hail within an updraft can be increased by a stagnation point just upstream the updraft. If the updraft is strong enough, the upper level flow will have to divert to either side of it, creating an area of little flow just behind the updraft. This area is favored for collection of condensation nuclei and thus can result in more hailstones if more of these nuclei make it into the updraft's hail growth area.

Downburst

Precipitation loading of the updraft can result from increased updraft strength too. Given the precipitation falls from a decent height, this can have the effect of dragging air to the surface, increasing strong wind (downburst) potential. To add to the downburst potential, a stronger updraft can more effectively entrain environmental dry air into the thunderstorm. This air would undergo evaporative cooling and become negatively buoyant, then would proceed to the earth's surface and create strong winds as they spread out along the surface. In more organized severe winds, the stronger updraft serves as the blockade to a rear inflow jet (RIJ), and can divert it to the surface to potentially create severe winds.

With regard to the thermodynamics of an updraft parcel, a downdraft parcel undergoes very similar changes. Both updraft and downdraft parcels experience temperature change at the dry adiabatic lapse rate of 9.8 C/KM, except decreasing for the former and increasing for the latter. The updraft parcel will have its dry adiabatic lapse rate moderated by the release of latent heat from moisture (adds heat to the dry adiabatic cooling), to the moist adiabatic lapse rate. This rate varies with moisture content, but will be warmer than its dry adiabatic counterpart. A downdraft, experiencing a temperature increase at the dry adiabatic lapse rate, will have that warming moderated by the absorption of latent heat from the rain it is accompanied by (just as the updraft does except for moderating the cooling with heat). This is only fully true for wet downbursts. Dry downbursts only experience this before hitting the ground.

An updraft begins convection at the Level of Free Convection (LFC), while a downdraft begins negatively convecting at the Level of Free Sink (LFS).

Tornadoes

There is still uncertainty regarding how tornadoes form, although it has been discovered that low level CAPE might increase tornado potential, especially in environments that wouldn't seem to be supportive of tornadoes. A parameter called Three CAPE (3CAPE), measures the CAPE in the lowest three kilometers of the atmosphere. Overall CAPE and a stronger updraft is important to maintaining a deep and persistent mid-level mesocyclone, which would be the parent mesocyclone to the tornado.

Measurement

The potential for convection in the atmosphere is often measured by an atmospheric temperature/dewpoint profile with height. This is often displayed on a Skew-T chart or other similar thermodynamic diagram. These can be plotted by a measured sounding analysis, which is the sending of a radiosonde attached to a balloon into the atmosphere to take the measurements with height. Forecast models can also create these diagrams, but are less accurate due to model uncertainties and biases, and have lower spatial resolution. Although, the temporal resolution of forecast model soundings is greater then the direct measurements, where the former can have plots for intervals of up to every 3 hours, and the latter as having only 2 per day (although when a convective event is expected a special sounding might be taken outside of the normal schedule of 00Z and then 12Z.)

Other Forecasting Concerns

Atmospheric convection can also be responsible for and have implications on a number of other weather conditions. A few examples on the smaller scale would include:

Convection mixing the planetary boundary layer (PBL) and allowing drier air aloft to the surface thereby decreasing dewpoints, creating cumulus type clouds which can limit a small amount of sunshine, increasing surface winds, making outflow boundaries/and other smaller boundaries more diffuse, and the eastward propagation of the dryline during the day. On the larger scale, rising of air can lead to warm core surface lows, often found in the desert southwest.

5

Earth's Atmosphere

Atmospheric gases scatter blue light more than other wavelengths, giving the Earth a blue halo when seen from spaceThe Earth's atmosphere (or air) is a layer of gases surrounding the planet Earth that is retained by the Earth's gravity. Dry air contains roughly (by volume) 78.08% nitrogen, 20.95% oxygen, 0.93% argon, 0.038% carbon dioxide, and trace amounts of other gases. Air also contains a variable amount of water vapor, on average around 1%. The atmosphere protects life on Earth by absorbing ultraviolet solar radiation, warming the surface through heat retention (greenhouse effect), and reducing temperature extremes between day and night.

There is no definite boundary between the atmosphere and outer space. It slowly becomes thinner and fades into space. An altitude of 120 km (75 mi) marks the boundary where atmospheric effects become noticeable during reentry. The Kármán line, at 100 km (62 mi), is also frequently regarded as the boundary between atmosphere and outer space. Three quarters of the atmosphere's mass is within 11 km (6.8 mi; 36,000 ft) of the surface.

Temperature and Layers

Layers of the Atmosphere

The temperature of the Earth's atmosphere varies with altitude; the mathematical relationship between temperature and altitude varies among five different atmospheric layers (ordered highest to lowest, the ionosphere is part of the thermosphere).

Exosphere

From 500-1,000 km (310-620 mi; 1,600,000-3,300,000 ft) up to 10,000 km (6,200 mi; 33,000,000 ft), contain free-moving particles that may migrate into and out of the magnetosphere or the solar wind.

Exobase

Also known as the 'critical level', it is the lower boundary of the exosphere.

Ionosphere

The part of the atmosphere that is ionized by solar radiation stretches from 50 to 1,000 km (31 to 620 mi; 160,000 to 3,300,000 ft) and typically overlaps both the exosphere and the thermosphere. It plays an important part in atmospheric electricity and forms the inner edge of the magnetosphere. Because of its charged particles, it has practical importance because it influences, for example, radio propagation on the Earth. It is responsible for auroras.

Thermopause

The boundary above the thermosphere, it varies in height from 500-1,000 km (310-620 mi; 1,600,000-3,300,000 ft).

Thermosphere

From 80-85 km (50-53 mi; 260,000-280,000 ft) to over 640 km (400 mi; 2,100,000 ft), temperature increasing with height. Although the temperature can rise to 1,500 °C (2,730 °F), a person would not feel warm because of the extremely low pressure. The International Space Station orbits in this layer, between 320 and 380 km (200 and 240 mi).

Mesopause

The temperature minimum at the boundary between the thermosphere and the mesosphere. It is the coldest place on Earth, with a temperature of -100 ºC (-148.0 ºF; 173.1 K).

Mesosphere

From the Greek word "µ?s??" meaning middle. The mesosphere extends from about 50 km (31 mi; 160,000 ft) to the range of 80-85 km (50-53 mi; 260,000-280,000 ft). Temperature decreases with height, reaching -100 ºC (-148.0 ºF; 173.1 K) in the upper mesosphere. This is also where most meteors burn up when entering the atmosphere.

Stratopause

The boundary between the mesosphere and the stratosphere, typically 50 to 55 km (31 to 34 mi; 160,000 to 180,000 ft). The pressure here is 1/1000th sea level.

Stratosphere

From the Latin word "stratus" meaning spreading out. The stratosphere extends from the troposphere's 7-17 km (4.3-11 mi; 23,000-56,000 ft) range to about 51 km (32 mi; 170,000 ft). Temperature increases with height. The stratosphere contains the ozone layer, the part of the Earth's atmosphere which contains relatively high concentrations of ozone. "Relatively high" means a few parts per million—much higher than the concentrations in the lower atmosphere but still small compared to the main components of the atmosphere. It is mainly located in the lower portion of the stratosphere from approximately 15-35 km (9.3-22 mi; 49,000-110,000 ft) above Earth's surface, though the thickness varies seasonally and geographically.

Ozone Layer

Though part of the Stratosphere, the ozone layer is considered as a layer of the Earth's atmosphere in itself because its physical and chemical composition is far different from the Stratosphere. Ozone (O_3) in the Earth's stratosphere is created by ultraviolet light striking oxygen molecules containing two oxygen atoms (O_2), splitting them into individual oxygen atoms (atomic oxygen); the atomic oxygen then combines with unbroken O_2 to create O_3. O_3 is unstable (although, in the stratosphere, long-lived) and when ultraviolet light hits ozone it splits into a molecule of O_2 and an atom of atomic oxygen, a continuing process called the ozone-oxygen cycle. This occurs in the ozone layer, the region from about 10 to 50 km (33,000 to 160,000 ft) above Earth's surface. About 90% of the ozone in our atmosphere is contained in the stratosphere. Ozone concentrations are greatest between about 20 and 40 km (66,000 and 130,000 ft), where they range from about 2 to 8 parts per million.

Tropopause

The boundary between the stratosphere and troposphere.

Troposphere

From the Greek word meaning to turn or change. The troposphere is the lowest layer of the atmosphere; it begins at the surface and extends to between 7 km (23,000 ft) at the poles and 17 km (56,000 ft) at the equator, with some variation due to weather factors. The troposphere has a great deal of vertical mixing because of solar heating at the area. This heating makes air masses less dense so they rise. When an air mass rises, the pressure upon it decreases so it expands, doing work against the opposing pressure of the surrounding air. To do work is to expend energy, so the temperature of the air mass decreases. As the temperature decreases, water vapor in the air mass may condense or solidify, releasing latent heat that further uplifts the air mass. This process determines the maximum rate of decline of temperature with height, called the adiabatic lapse rate. The troposphere contains roughly 80% of the total mass of the atmosphere. Fifty percent of the total mass of the atmosphere is located in the lower 5.6 km (18,000 ft) of the troposphere.

The average temperature of the atmosphere at the surface of Earth is 20 °C (68 °F; 293 K).

Pressure and Thickness

The average atmospheric pressure, at sea level, is about 101.3 kilopascals (14.69 psi); total atmospheric mass is 5.1480 × 1018 kg (1.135 × 1019 lb)

Atmospheric pressure is a direct result of the total weight of the air above the point at which the pressure is measured. Air pressure varies with location and time, because the amount (and weight) of air above the earth varies with location and time. However, the average mass of the air above a square meter of the Earth's surface can be calculated from the total amount of air and the surface area of the Earth. The total air mass is 5148.0 teratonnes and area is 51007.2 megahectares. Thus 5148.0/510.072 = 10.093 tonnes (9.934 LT; 11.126 ST) per square meter or 14.356 pounds per square inch (98.98 kPa). This is about 2.5% below the officially standardized unit atmosphere (1 atm) of 101.325 kPa or 14.696 psi, and corresponds to the mean pressure not at sea level, but at the mean base of the atmosphere as contoured by the Earth's terrain.

Were atmospheric density to remain constant with height the atmosphere would terminate abruptly at 7.81 km (25,600 ft). Instead, density decreases with height, dropping by 50% at an altitude of about 5.6 km (18,000 ft). For comparison the highest mountain, Mount Everest, is higher, at 8.8 km (29,000 ft), so air is less than half as dense at the summit than at sea level. This is why it is so difficult to climb without supplemental oxygen.

This pressure drop is approximately exponential, so that pressure decreases by approximately half every 5.6 km (18,000 ft) and by 63.2% (1 - 1 / e = 1 - 0.368 = 0.632) every 7.64 km (25,100 ft), the average scale height of Earth's atmosphere below 70 km (43 mi; 230,000 ft). However, because of changes in temperature, average molecular weight, and gravity throughout the atmospheric column, the dependence of atmospheric pressure on altitude is modeled by separate equations for each of the layers listed above. Even in the exosphere, the atmosphere is still present. This can be seen by the effects of atmospheric drag on satellites.

In summary, the equations of pressure by altitude in the above references can be used directly to estimate atmospheric thickness. However, the following published data are given for reference:

- 50% of the atmosphere by mass is below an altitude of 5.6 km (18,000 ft).
- 90% of the atmosphere by mass is below an altitude of 16 km (52,000 ft). The common altitude of commercial airliners is about 10 km (33,000 ft) and Mt. Everest's summit is 8,848 m (29,030 ft) above sea level.
- 99.99997% of the atmosphere by mass is below 100 km (62 mi; 330,000 ft), although in the rarefied region above this there are auroras and other atmospheric effects. The highest X-15 plane flight in 1963 reached an altitude of 354,300 ft (108.0 km).

Composition

Composition of Earth's atmosphere as of Dec. 1987. The lower pie represents the least common gases that compose 0.038% of the atmosphere. Values normalized for illustration.

Filtered air includes trace amounts of many of the chemical elements. Substantial amounts of argon, nitrogen, and oxygen are present as elementary gases. Note the major greenhouse gasses: water vapor, carbon dioxide, methane, nitrous oxide, and ozone. Many additional elements from natural sources may be present in tiny amounts in an unfiltered air sample, including contributions from dust, pollen and spores, sea spray, vulcanism, and meteoroids. Various industrial pollutants are also now present in the air, such as chlorine (elementary or in compounds), fluorine (in compounds), elementary mercury, and sulfur (in compounds such as sulfur dioxide [SO_2]).

ppmv

The parts per million by volume (pp mv) figures above are by volume-fraction (V%), which for ideal gases is equal to mole-fraction (that is, the fraction of total molecules). Although the atmosphere is not an ideal gas, nonetheless the atmosphere behaves enough like an ideal gas that the volume-fraction is the same as the mole-fraction for the precision given.

By contrast, mass-fraction abundances of gases will differ from the volume values. The mean molar mass of air is 28.97 g/mol, while the molar mass of helium is 4.00, and krypton is 83.80. Thus helium is 5.2 ppm by volume-fraction, but 0.72 ppm by mass-fraction ([4/29] × 5.2 = 0.72), and krypton is 1.1 ppm by volume-fraction, but 3.2 ppm by mass-fraction × 1.1 = 3.2).

Heterosphere

Below the turbopause, at an altitude of about 100 km (62 mi; 330,000 ft) (not far from the mesopause), the Earth's atmosphere has a more-or-less uniform composition (apart from water vapor) as described above; this constitutes the homosphere However, above the turbopause, the Earth's atmosphere begins to have a composition which varies with altitude. This is because, in the absence of mixing, the density of a gas falls off exponentially with increasing altitude but at a rate which depends on the molar mass. Thus higher mass constituents, such as oxygen and nitrogen, fall off more quickly than lighter constituents such as helium and hydrogen. Thus there is a layer, called the heterosphere, in which the Earth's atmosphere has varying composition. The precise altitude of the heterosphere and the layers it contains varies significantly with temperature.

Density and Mass

Temperature and mass density against altitude from the NRLMSISE-00 standard atmosphere model.

Density of Air

The density of air at sea level is about 1.2 kg/m^3 (1.2 g/L). Natural variations of the barometric pressure occur at any one altitude as a consequence of weather. This variation is relatively small for inhabited altitudes but much more pronounced in the outer atmosphere and space because of variable solar radiation.

The atmospheric density decreases as the altitude increases. This variation can be approximately modeled using the barometric formula. More sophisticated models are used by meteorologists and space agencies to predict weather and orbital decay of satellites.

The average mass of the atmosphere is about 5 quadrillion metric tons or 1/1,200,000 the mass of Earth. According to the National Center for Atmospheric Research, "The total mean mass of the atmosphere is 5.1480×10^{18} kg with an annual range due to water vapor of 1.2 or 1.5×10^{15} kg depending on whether surface pressure or water vapor data are used; somewhat smaller than the previous estimate. The mean mass of water vapor is estimated as 1.27×10^{16} kg and the dry air mass as $5.1352 \pm 0.0003 \times 10^{18}$ kg."

Opacity

Earth's atmosphere from space. The blue and red of the atmosphere is due to Rayleigh scattering; shorter (blue) wavelengths of light are scattered more easily than longer (red) wavelengths.

Solar radiation (or sunlight) is the energy the Earth receives from the Sun. The Earth also emits radiation back into space, but at longer wavelengths that we cannot see. Depending on its condition, the atmosphere can block radiation from coming in or going out. Important examples of this are clouds and the greenhouse effect.

Scattering

When light passes through our atmosphere, photons interact with it through scattering. If the light does not interact with the atmosphere, it is called direct radiation and is what you see if you were to look directly at the sun. Indirect radiation is light that has been scattered in the atmosphere. For example, on an overcast day when you can't see your shadow there is no direct radiation reaching you, it has all been scattered. As another example, due to a phenomenon called Rayleigh scattering, shorter (blue) wavelengths scatter more easily than longer (red) wavelengths. This is why the sky looks blue, you are seeing scattered blue light. This is also why sunsets are red. Because the sun is close to the horizon, the sun rays pass through more atmosphere than normal to reach your eye. All of the blue light has been scattered out, leaving the red light in a sunset.

Absorption

Absorption is another important property of the atmosphere. Different molecules absorb different wavelengths of radiation. For example, O_2 and O_3 absorb almost all wavelengths shorter than 300 nanometers. Water (H_2O) absorbs many wavelengths above 700 nm, but this depends on the amount of water vapor in the atmosphere. When a molecule absorbs a photon, it increases the energy of the molecule. We can think of this as heating the atmosphere, but the atmosphere also cools by emitting radiation, as discussed below.

Rough plot of Earth's atmospheric transmittance (or opacity) to various wavelengths of electromagnetic radiation, including visible light.

When you combine the absorption spectra of the gasses in the atmosphere, you are left with "windows" of low opacity, allowing the transmission of only certain bands of light. The optical window runs from around 300 nm (ultraviolet-C) up into the range humans can see, the visible spectrum (commonly called light), at roughly 400-700 nm and continues to the infrared to around 1100 nm. There are also infrared and radio windows that transmit some infrared and radio waves at longer wavelengths. For example, the radio window runs from about one centimeter to about eleven-meter waves.

Emission (Electromagnetic Radiation)

Emission is the opposite of absorption, it is when an object emits radiation. Objects tend to emit amounts and wavelengths of radiation depending on their "black body" emission curves, therefore hotter objects tend to emit more radiation at shorter wavelengths. Colder objects emit less radiation at longer wavelengths. For example, the sun is approximately 6,000 K (5,730 °C; 10,340 °F), its radiation peaks near 500 nm, and is visible to the human eye. The Earth is approximately 290 K (17 °C; 62 °F), so its radiation peaks near 10,000 nm, and is much too long to be visible by humans.

Because of its temperature, the atmosphere emits infrared radiation. For example, on clear nights the Earth's surface cools down faster than on cloudy nights. This is because clouds (H_2O) are strong absorbers and emitters of infrared radiation. This is also why it becomes colder at night at higher elevations. The atmosphere acts as a "blanket" to limit the amount of radiation the Earth loses into space.

The greenhouse effect is directly related to this absorption and emission (or "blanket") effect. Some chemicals in the atmosphere absorb and emit infrared radiation, but do not interact with sunlight in the visible spectrum. Common examples of these chemicals are CO_2 and H_2O. If there are too much of these greenhouse gasses, sunlight heats the Earth's surface, but the gasses block the infrared radiation from exiting back to space. This imbalance causes the Earth to warm, and thus climate change.

Atmospheric Circulation

Atmospheric circulation is the large-scale movement of air, and the means (with ocean circulation) by which heat is distributed on the surface of the Earth.

The large-scale structure of the atmospheric circulation varies from year to year, but the basic structure remains fairly constant. However, individual weather systems -

midlatitude depressions, or tropical convective cells - occur "randomly". It is accepted that weather cannot be predicted beyond a fairly short limit; perhaps a month in theory, or about ten days in practice. Nonetheless, the average of these systems (the climate) is stable over longer periods of time.

Evolution of Earth's Atmosphere

The history of the Earth's atmosphere prior to one billion years ago is poorly understood; it is an active area of scientific research. The following discussion presents a plausible scenario.

The modern atmosphere is sometimes referred to as Earth's "third atmosphere", in order to distinguish the current chemical composition from previous compositions. The original atmosphere was primarily helium and hydrogen. Heat from the still-molten crust, the sun, and a probably enhanced solar wind, dissipated this atmosphere.

About 4.4 billion years ago, the surface had cooled enough to form a crust. It was heavily populated with volcanoes which released steam, carbon dioxide, and ammonia. This led to the early "second atmosphere", which was primarily carbon dioxide and water vapor, with some nitrogen but virtually no oxygen. This second atmosphere had approximately 100 times as much gas as the current atmosphere, but as it cooled much of the carbon dioxide was dissolved in the seas and precipitated out as carbonates. The later "second atmosphere" contained largely nitrogen and carbon dioxide. However, simulations run at the University of Waterloo and University of Colorado in 2005 suggest that it may have had up to 40% hydrogenIt is generally believed that the greenhouse effect, caused by high levels of carbon dioxide and methane, kept the Earth from freezing.

One of the earliest types of bacteria was the cyanobacteria, which formed into colonies called stromatolites. Fossil evidence indicates that bacteria shaped like these existed approximately 3.3 billion years ago and were the first oxygen-producing evolving phototropic organisms. They were responsible for the initial conversion of the Earth's atmosphere from an anoxic state to an oxic state (that is, from a state without oxygen to a state with oxygen) during the period 2.7 to 2.2 billion years ago. Being the first to carry out oxygenic photosynthesis, they were able to produce oxygen while sequestering carbon dioxide in organic molecules, playing a major role in oxygenating the atmosphere. This is often referred to as the Oxygen Catastrophe. The increase in the concentration of oxygen in the atmosphere required time because iron and other elements in the Earth's crust reacted with oxygen, removing it from the atmosphere.

Photosynthesising plants later evolved and continued releasing oxygen and sequestering carbon dioxide. Over time, excess carbon became locked in fossil fuels, sedimentary rocks (notably limestone), and animal shells. As oxygen was released, it reacted with ammonia to release nitrogen. Bacteria also converted ammonia into nitrogen, but most of the nitrogen currently in the atmosphere resulted from sunlight-powered photolysis of ammonia released steadily over the aeons from volcanoes.

As more plants appeared, the levels of oxygen increased significantly, while carbon dioxide levels dropped. At first the oxygen combined with various elements, but eventually oxygen accumulated in the atmosphere, contributing to Cambrian explosion and further evolution. With the appearance of an ozone layer (ozone is an allotrope of oxygen) life-forms were better protected from ultraviolet radiation. This oxygen-nitrogen atmosphere is the "third atmosphere". Between 200 and 250 million years ago, up to 35% of the atmosphere was oxygen (as found in bubbles of ancient atmosphere preserved in amber).

This modern atmosphere has a composition which is enforced by oceanic blue-green algae as well as geological processes. O_2 does not remain naturally free in an atmosphere but tends to be consumed by inorganic chemical reactions, and by animals, bacteria, and even land plants at night. CO_2 tends to be produced by respiration and decomposition and oxidation of organic matter. Due to this, O_2 would vanish within a few million years by chemical reactions, and CO_2 dissolves in water and would be gone in millennia if not replaced. Both are maintained by biological productivity and geological forces seemingly working hand-in-hand to maintain reasonably steady levels over millions of years.

Currently, anthropogenic greenhouse gases are increasing in the atmosphere and this is a causative factor in global warming

Air Pollution

Before desulfurization filters were installed, the emissions from this power plant in New Mexico contained excessive amounts of sulfur dioxide.

Air pollution is the human introduction of chemicals, particulate matter, or biological materials that cause harm or discomfort to organisms, into the atmosphere Stratospheric ozone depletion is believed to be caused by air pollution (chiefly from chlorofluorocarbons).

Worldwide, air pollution is responsible for large numbers of deaths and respiratory disease. Enforced air quality standards, like the Clean Air Act in the United States, have reduced the presence of some pollutants. While major stationary sources are often identified with air pollution, the greatest source of emissions is actually mobile sources, principally the automobile Gases such as carbon dioxide, methane, and fluorocarbons contribute to global warming, and these gases, or excess amounts of some emitted from fossil fuel burning, have recently been identified by the United States and many other countries as pollutants.

ATMOSPHERIC CHEMISTRY

Atmospheric chemistry is a branch of atmospheric science in which the chemistry of the Earth's atmosphere and that of other planets is studied. It is a multidisciplinary field of research and draws on environmental chemistry, physics, meteorology, computer modeling, oceanography, geology and volcanology and other disciplines. Research is increasingly connected with other areas of study such as climatology.

The composition and chemistry of the atmosphere is of importance for several reasons, but primarily because of the interactions between the atmosphere and living organisms. The composition of the Earth's atmosphere has been changed by human activity and some of these changes are harmful to human health, crops and ecosystems. Examples of problems which have been addressed by atmospheric chemistry include acid rain, photochemical smog and global warming. Atmospheric chemistry seeks to understand the causes of these problems, and by obtaining a theoretical understanding of them, allow possible solutions to be tested and the effects of changes in government policy evaluated.

History

The ancient Greeks regarded air as one of the four elements, but the first scientific studies of atmospheric composition began in the 18th century. Chemists such as Joseph Priestley, Antoine Lavoisier and Henry Cavendish made the first measurements of the composition of the atmosphere.

In the late 19th and early 20th centuries interest shifted towards trace constituents with very small concentrations. One particularly important discovery for atmospheric chemistry was the discovery of ozone by Christian Friedrich Schoenbein in 1840.

In the 20th century atmospheric science moved on from studying the composition of air to a consideration of how the concentrations of trace gases in the atmosphere have changed over time and the chemical processes which create and destroy compounds in the air. Two particularly important examples of this were the explanation of how the ozone layer is created and maintained by Sydney Chapman and Gordon Dobson, and the explanation of Photochemical smog by Haagen-Smit.

In the 21st century the focus is now shifting again. Atmospheric Chemistry is increasingly studied as one part of the Earth system. Instead of concentrating on atmospheric chemistry in isolation the focus is now on seeing it as one part of a single system with the rest of the atmosphere, biosphere and geosphere. An especially important driver for this is the links between chemistry and climate such as the effects of changing climate on the recovery of the ozone hole and vice versa but also interaction of the composition of the atmosphere with the oceans and terrestrial ecosystems.

Methodology

Observations, lab measurements and modelling are the three central elements in atmospheric chemistry. Progress in atmospheric chemistry is often driven by the interactions between these components and they form an integrated whole. For example observations may tell us that more of a chemical compound exists than previously thought possible. This will stimulate new modelling and laboratory studies which will increase our scientific understanding to a point where the observations can be explained.

Observation

Observations of atmospheric chemistry are essential to our understanding. Routine observations of chemical composition tell us about changes in atmospheric composition over time. One important example of this is the Keeling Curve - a series of measurements from 1958 to today which show a steady rise in of the concentration of carbon dioxide.

Observations of atmospheric chemistry are made in observatories such as that on Mauna Loa and on mobile platforms such as aircraft (e.g. the UK's Facility for Airborne Atmospheric Measurements), ships and balloons. Observations of atmospheric composition are increasingly made by satellites with important instruments such as GOME and MOPITT giving a global picture of air pollution and chemistry. Surface observations have the advantage that they provide long term records at high time resolution but are limited in the vertical and horizontal space they provide observations from. Some surface based instruments e.g. LIDAR can provide concentration profiles of chemical compounds and aerosol but are still restricted in the horizontal region they can cover. Many observations are available on line in Atmospheric Chemistry Observational Databases.

Lab Measurements

Measurements made in the laboratory are essential to our understanding of the sources and sinks of pollutants and naturally occurring compounds. Lab studies tell us which gases react with each other and how fast they react. Measurements of interest include reactions in the gas phase, on surfaces and in water. Also of high importance is photochemistry which quantifies how quickly molecules are split apart by sunlight and what the products are plus thermodynamic data such as Henry's law coefficients.

Modelling

In order to synthesise and test theoretical understanding of atmospheric chemistry, computer models (such as chemical transport models) are used. Numerical models solve the differential equations governing the concentrations of chemicals in the atmosphere. They can be very simple or very complicated. One common trade off in numerical models is between the number of chemical compounds and chemical reactions modelled versus the representation of transport and mixing in the atmosphere. For example, a box model might include hundreds or even thousands of chemical reactions but will only have a very crude representation of mixing in the atmosphere. In contrast, 3D models represent many of the physical processes of the atmosphere but due to constraints on computer resources will have far fewer chemical reactions and compounds. Models can be used to interpret observations, test understanding of chemical reactions and predict future concentrations of chemical compounds in the atmosphere. One important current trend is for atmospheric chemistry modules to become one part of earth system models in which the links between climate, atmospheric composition and the biosphere can be studied.

Some models are constructed by automatic code generators. In this approach a set of constituents are chosen and the automatic code generator will then select the reactions involving those constituents from a set of reaction databases. Once the reactions have been chosen the ordinary differential equations (ODE) that describe their time evolution can be automatically constructed.

ATMOSPHERIC SCIENCES

Atmospheric sciences is an umbrella term for the study of the atmosphere, its processes, the effects other systems have on the atmosphere, and the effects of the atmosphere on these other systems. Meteorology includes atmospheric chemistry and atmospheric physics with a major focus on weather forecasting. Climatology is the study of atmospheric changes (both long and short-term) that define average climates and their change over time, due to both natural and anthropogenic climate variability. Aeronomy is the study of the upper layers of the atmosphere, where dissociation and ionization are important. Atmospheric science has been extended to the field of planetary science and the study of the atmospheres of the planets of the solar system.

Atmospheric Dynamics

Atmospheric dynamics involves the study of observations and theory dealing with all motion systems of meteorological importance. The list includes diverse phenomena as thunderstorms, tornadoes, gravity waves, tropical cyclones, extratropical cyclones, jet streams, and global-scale circulations. The goal of dynamical studies is to explain the observed circulations on the basis of fundamental principles from physics. The objectives of such studies include improving weather forecasting, developing methods for predicting seasonal and interannual climate fluctuations, and understanding the implications of human-induced perturbations (e.g., increased carbon dioxide concentrations or depletion of the ozone layer) on the global climate.

Atmospheric Physics

Atmospheric physics is the application of physics to the study of the atmosphere. Atmospheric physicists attempt to model Earth's atmosphere and the atmospheres of the other planets using fluid flow equations, chemical models, radiation balancing, and energy transfer processes in the atmosphere and underlying oceans. In order to model weather systems, atmospheric physicists employ elements of scattering theory, wave propagation models, cloud physics, statistical mechanics and spatial statistics which are highly mathematical and related to physics. It has close links to meteorology and climatology and also covers the design and construction of instruments for studying the atmosphere and the interpretation of the data they provide, including remote sensing instruments.

In the UK, atmospheric studies are underpinned by the Meteorological Office. Divisions of the U.S. National Oceanic and Atmospheric Administration (NOAA) oversee research projects and weather modeling involving atmospheric physics. The U.S. National Astronomy and Ionosphere Center also carries out studies of the high atmosphere.

In contrast to meteorology, which studies short term weather systems lasting up to a few weeks, climatology studies the frequency and trends of those systems. It studies the periodicity of weather events over years to millennia, as well as changes in long-term average weather patterns, in relation to atmospheric conditions. Climatologists, those who practice climatology, study both the nature of climates - local, regional or global - and the natural or human-induced factors that cause climates to change. Climatology considers the past and can help predict future climate change.

Phenomena of climatological interest include the atmospheric boundary layer, circulation patterns, heat transfer (radiative, convective and latent), interactions between the atmosphere and the oceans and land surface (particularly vegetation, land use and topography), and the chemical and physical composition of the atmosphere. Related disciplines include astrophysics, atmospheric physics, chemistry, ecology, geology, geophysics, glaciology, hydrology, oceanography, and volcanology.

Atmospheres on Other Planets

All of the Solar System planets have atmospheres as their large masses mean gravity is strong enough to keep gaseous particles close to the surface. The larger gas giants are massive enough to keep large amounts of the light gases hydrogen and helium close by, while the smaller planets lose these gases into space. The composition of the Earth's atmosphere is different from the other planets because the various life processes that have transpired on the planet have introduced free molecular oxygen The only solar planet without a true atmosphere is Mercury which had it mostly, although not entirely, blasted away by the solar wind.

Planetary atmospheres are affected by the varying degrees of energy received from either the Sun or their interiors, leading to the formation of dynamic weather systems such as hurricanes, (on Earth), planet-wide dust storms (on Mars), an Earth-sized anticyclone on Jupiter (called the Great Red Spot), and holes in the atmosphere (on Neptune) At least one extrasolar planet, HD 189733 b, has been claimed to possess such a weather system, similar to the Great Red Spot but twice as large.

Hot Jupiters have been shown to be losing their atmospheres into space due to stellar radiation, much like the tails of comets. These planets may have vast differences in temperature between their day and night sides which produce supersonic winds, although the day and night sides of HD 189733b appear to have very similar temperatures, indicating that that planet's atmosphere effectively redistributes the star's energy around the planet.

6

ACID RAIN

Acid rain is rain or any other form of precipitation that is unusually acidic. It has harmful effects on plants, aquatic animals, and infrastructure. Acid rain is mostly caused by human emissions of sulfur and nitrogen compounds which react in the atmosphere to produce acids. In recent years, many governments have introduced laws to reduce these emissions.

Definition

"Acid rain" is a popular term referring to the deposition of wet (rain, snow, sleet, fog and cloudwater, dew) and dry (acidifying particles and gases) acidic components. A more accurate term is "acid deposition". Distilled water, which contains no carbon dioxide, has a neutral pH of 7. Liquids with a pH less than 7 are acidic, and those with a pH greater than 7 are basic. "Clean" or unpolluted rain has a slightly acidic pH of about 5.2, because carbon dioxide and water in the air react together to form carbonic acid, a weak acid (pH 5.6 in distilled water), but unpolluted rain also contains other chemicals.

$$H_2O\ (l) + CO_2\ (g) \rightarrow H_2CO_3\ (aq)$$

Carbonic acid then can ionize in water forming low concentrations of hydronium ions:

$$2H_2O\ (l) + H_2CO_3\ (aq) \rightleftharpoons CO_3^{2-}\ (ag) + 2H_3O^+(aq)$$

The extra acidity in rain comes from the reaction of primary air pollutants, primarily sulfur oxides and nitrogen oxides, with water in the air to form strong acids (like sulfuric and nitric acid). The main sources of these pollutants are industrial power-generating plants and vehicles.

History

Since the Industrial Revolution, emissions of sulphur dioxide and nitrogen oxides to the atmosphere have increased. In 1852, Robert Angus Smith was the first to show the relationship between acid rain and atmospheric pollution in Manchester, England Though acidic rain was discovered in 1852, it wasn't until the late 1960s that scientists began widely observing and studying the phenomenon. The term "acid rain" was generated in 1972 Canadian Harold Harvey was among the first to research a "dead" lake. Public awareness of acid rain in the U.S increased in the 1970s after the New York Times promulgated reports from the Hubbard Brook Experimental Forest in New Hampshire of the myriad deleterious environmental effects demonstrated to result from it.

Occasional pH readings in rain and fog water of well below 2.4 (the acidity of vinegar) have been reported in industrialized areas Industrial acid rain is a substantial problem in Europe, China Russia and areas down-wind from them. These areas all burn sulfur-containing coal to generate heat and electricity. The problem of acid rain not only has increased with population and industrial growth, but has become more widespread. The use of tall smokestacks to reduce local pollution has contributed to the spread of acid rain by releasing gases into regional atmospheric circulation Often deposition occurs a considerable distance downwind of the emissions, with mountainous regions tending to receive the greatest deposition (simply because of their higher rainfall). An example of this effect is the low pH of rain (compared to the local emissions) which falls in Scandinavia.

Emissions of Chemicals Leading to Acidification

The most important gas which leads to acidification is sulfur dioxide. Emissions of nitrogen oxides which are oxidized to form nitric acid are of increasing importance due to stricter controls on emissions of sulfur containing compounds. 70 Tg(S) per year in the form of SO_2 comes from fossil fuel combustion and industry, 2.8 Tg(S) from wildfires and 7-8 Tg(S) per year from volcanoes

Natural Phenomena

The principal natural phenomena that contribute acid-producing gases to the atmosphere are emissions from volcanoes and those from biological processes that occur on the land, in wetlands, and in the oceans. The major biological source of sulfur containing compounds is dimethyl sulfide.

Acidic deposits have been detected in glacial ice thousands of years old in remote parts of the globe.

Human Activity

The principal cause of acid rain is sulfur and nitrogen compounds from human sources, such as electricity generation, factories, and motor vehicles. Coal power plants are one of the most polluting. The gases can be carried hundreds of kilometres in the atmosphere before they are converted to acids and deposited. In the past, factories had short funnels to let out smoke, but this caused many problems locally; thus, factories now have taller smoke funnels. However, dispersal from these taller stacks causes pollutants to be carried farther, causing widespread ecological damage.

Gas Phase Chemistry

In the gas phase sulfur dioxide is oxidized by reaction with the hydroxyl radical via an inter-molecular reaction:

$SO_2 + OH \rightarrow HOSO_2$

which is followed by:

$HOSO_2 + O_2 \rightarrow HO_2 + SO_3$

In the presence of water, sulfur trioxide (SO_3) is converted rapidly to sulfuric acid:

$SO_3(g) + H_2O(l) \rightarrow H_2SO_4(l)$

Nitric acid is formed by the reaction of OH with nitrogen dioxide:

$NO_2 + OH \rightarrow HNO_3$

Chemistry in Cloud Droplets

When clouds are present the loss rate of SO_2 is faster than can be explained by gas phase chemistry alone. This is due to reactions in the liquid water droplets.

Hydrolysis

Sulfur dioxide dissolves in water and then, like carbon dioxide, hydrolyses in a series of equilibrium reactions:

$SO_2\,(g) + H_2O \rightleftharpoons SO_2\,H_2O$

$SO_2\,H_2O \rightleftharpoons H^+ + HSO_3^-$

$HSO_3^- \rightleftharpoons H^+ + SO_3^{2-}$

Oxidation

There are a large number of aqueous reactions that oxidize sulfur from S(IV) to S(VI), leading to the formation of sulfuric acid. The most important oxidation reactions are with ozone, hydrogen peroxide and oxygen (reactions with oxygen are catalyzed by iron and manganese in the cloud droplets).

Acid Deposition

Processes involved in acid deposition (note that only SO_2 and NO_x play a significant role in acid rain).

Wet Deposition

Wet deposition of acids occurs when any form of precipitation (rain, snow, etc.) removes acids from the atmosphere and delivers it to the Earth's surface. This can result from the deposition of acids produced in the raindrops (see aqueous phase chemistry above) or by the precipitation removing the acids either in clouds or below clouds. Wet removal of both gases and aerosols are both of importance for wet deposition.

Dry Deposition

Acid deposition also occurs via dry deposition in the absence of precipitation. This can be responsible for as much as 20 to 60% of total acid deposition This occurs when particles and gases stick to the ground, plants or other surfaces.

Adverse Effects

Acid rain has been shown to have adverse impacts on forests, freshwaters and soils, killing insect and aquatic life-forms as well as causing damage to buildings and having impacts on human health.

Surface Waters and Aquatic Animals

Both the lower pH and higher aluminum concentrations in surface water that occur as a result of acid rain can cause damage to fish and other aquatic animals. At pHs lower than 5 most fish eggs will not hatch and lower pHs can kill adult fish. As lakes and rivers become more acidic biodiversity is reduced. Acid rain has eliminated insect life and some fish species, including the brook trout in some lakes, streams, and creeks in geographically sensitive areas, such as the Adirondack Mountains of the United States. However, the extent to which acid rain contributes directly or indirectly via runoff from the catchment to lake and river acidity (i.e., depending on characteristics of the surrounding watershed) is variable. The United States Environmental Protection Agency?'s (EPA) website states: "Of the lakes and streams surveyed, acid rain caused acidity in 75 percent of the acidic lakes and about 50 percent of the acidic streams".

Soils

Soil biology and chemistry can be seriously damaged by acid rain. Some microbes are unable to tolerate changes to low pHs and are killed. The enzymes of these microbes are denatured (changed in shape so they no longer function) by the acid. The hydronium ions of acid rain also mobilize toxins, e.g. aluminium, and leach away essential nutrients and minerals.

$$2H^{+}\,(aq) + Mg^{2+}\,(clay \rightleftharpoons 2H^{+}\,(clay) + Mg^{2+}(aq)$$

Soil chemistry can be dramatically changed when base cations, such as calcium and magnesium, are leached by acid rain thereby affecting sensitive species, such as sugar maple (Acer saccharum)

Forests and Other Vegetation

Adverse effects may be indirectly related to acid rain, like the acid's effects on soil or high concentration of gaseous precursors to acid rain. High altitude forests are especially vulnerable as they are often surrounded by clouds and fog which are more acidic than rain.

Other plants can also be damaged by acid rain but the effect on food crops is minimized by the application of lime and fertilizers to replace lost nutrients. In cultivated areas, limestone may also be added to increase the ability of the soil to keep the pH stable, but this tactic is largely unusable in the case of wilderness lands. When calcium is leached from the needles of red spruce, these trees become less cold tolerant and exhibit winter injury and even death.

Human Health

Scientists have suggested direct links to human health. Fine particles, a large fraction of which are formed from the same gases as acid rain (sulfur dioxide and nitrogen dioxide), have been shown to cause illness and premature deaths such as cancer and other diseases. For more information on the health effects of aerosols see particulate health effects.

Other Adverse Effects

Acid rain can also cause damage to certain building materials and historical monuments. This results when the sulfuric acid in the rain chemically reacts with the calcium compounds in the stones (limestone, sandstone, marble and granite) to create gypsum, which then flakes off.

$$CaCO_3\ (s) + H_2SO_4\ (aq) \rightleftharpoons CaSO_4\ (aq) + CO_2\ (g) + H_2O\ (l)$$

This result is also commonly seen on old gravestones where the acid rain can cause the inscription to become completely illegible. Acid rain also causes an increased rate of oxidation for iron Visibility is also reduced by sulfate and nitrate aerosols and particles in the atmosphere.

Affected Areas

Particularly badly affected places around the globe include most of Europe (particularly Scandinavia with many lakes with acidic water containing no life and many trees dead) many parts of the United States (states like New York are very badly affected) and South Western Canada. Other affected areas include the South Eastern coast of China and Taiwan.

Potential Problem Areas in the Future

Places like much of South Asia (Indonesia, Malaysia and Thailand), Western South Africa (the country), Southern India and Sri Lanka and even West Africa (countries like Ghana, Togo and Nigeria) could all be prone to acidic rainfall in the future.

Prevention Methods

Technical Solutions

In the United States, many coal-burning power plants use Flue gas desulfurization (FGD) to remove sulfur-containing gases from their stack gases. An example of FGD is the wet scrubber which is commonly used in the U.S. and many other countries. A wet scrubber is basically a reaction tower equipped with a fan that extracts hot smoke stack gases from a power plant into the tower. Lime or limestone in slurry form is also injected into the tower to mix with the stack gases and combine with the sulfur dioxide present. The calcium carbonate of the limestone produces pH-neutral calcium sulfate that is physically removed from the scrubber. That is, the scrubber turns sulfur pollution into industrial sulfates.

In some areas the sulfates are sold to chemical companies as gypsum when the purity of calcium sulfate is high. In others, they are placed in landfill. However, the effects of acid rain can last for generations, as the effects of pH level change can stimulate the continued leaching of undesirable chemicals into otherwise pristine water sources, killing off vulnerable insect and fish species and blocking efforts to restore native life.

Automobile emissions control reduces emissions of nitrogen oxides from motor vehicles.

International Treaties

A number of international treaties on the long range transport of atmospheric pollutants have been agreed e.g. Sulphur Emissions Reduction Protocol under the Convention on Long-Range Transboundary Air Pollution.

Emission Trading

In this regulatory scheme, every current polluting facility is given or may purchase on an open market an emissions allowance for each unit of a designated pollutant it emits. Operators can then install pollution control equipment, and sell portions of their emissions allowances they no longer need for their own operations, thereby recovering some of the capital cost of their investment in such equipment. The intention is to give operators economic incentives to install pollution controls.

The first emissions trading market was established in the United States by enactment of the Clean Air Act Amendments of 1990. The overall goal of the Acid Rain Program established by the Act is to achieve significant environmental and public health benefits through reductions in emissions of sulfur dioxide (SO_2) and nitrogen oxides (NO_x), the primary causes of acid rain. To achieve this goal at the lowest cost to society, the program employs both regulatory and market based approaches for controlling air pollution.

7

Climate Change

Climate change is any long-term significant change in the expected patterns of average weather of a specific region (or, more relevantly to contemporary socio-political concerns, of the Earth as a whole) over an appropriately significant period of time. Climate change reflects abnormal variations to the expected climate within the Earth's atmosphere and subsequent effects on other parts of the Earth, such as in the ice caps over durations ranging from decades to millions of years.

In the context of environmental policy, climate change usually refers to changes in modern climate. For information on temperature measurements over various periods, and the data sources available, see temperature record. For attribution of climate change over the past century, see attribution of recent climate change.

Climate Change Factors

Climate Change is the result of a great many factors including the dynamic processes of the Earth itself, external forces including variations in sunlight intensity, and more recently by human activities. External factors that can shape climate are often called climate forcings and include such processes as variations in solar radiation, deviations in the Earth's orbit, and the level of greenhouse gas concentrations.

Glaciation

Glaciers are recognized as being among the most sensitive indicators of climate change, advancing during climate cooling (for example, during the period known as the Little Ice Age) and retreating during climate warming on moderate time scales. Glaciers grow and collapse, both contributing to natural variability and greatly amplifying externally forced changes. A world glacier inventory has been compiled since the 1970s. Initially based mainly on aerial photographs and maps, this compilation has resulted in a detailed inventory of more than 100,000 glaciers covering a total area of approximately 240,000 km^2 and, in preliminary estimates, for the recording of the remaining ice cover estimated to be around 445,000 km^2. From this data, glaciers worldwide have been shown to be shrinking significantly, with strong glacier retreats in the 1940s, stable or growing conditions during the 1920s and 1970s, and again increasing rates of ice loss from the mid 1980s to present.

The most significant climate processes of the last several million years are the glacial and interglacial cycles of the present age. The present interglaciation (often termed the Holocene) has lasted about 10,000 years Shaped by orbital variations, earth-based responses such as the rise and fall of continental ice sheets and significant sea-level changes helped create the climate. Other changes, including Heinrich events, Dansgaard–Oeschger events and the Younger Dryas, however, illustrate how glacial variations may also influence climate without the forcing effect of orbital changes.

Thermohaline Circulation

On a timescale often measured in decades or more, climate changes can also result from the interaction between the atmosphere and the oceans. Many climate fluctuations, including the El Niño Southern oscillation, the Pacific decadal oscillation, the North Atlantic oscillation, and the Arctic oscillation, owe their existence at least in part to the different ways that heat may be stored in the oceans and also to the way it moves between various 'reservoirs'. On longer time scales (with a complete cycle often taking up to a thousand years to complete), ocean processes such as thermohaline circulation also play a key role in redistributing heat by carrying out a very slow and extremely deep movement of water, and the long-term redistribution of heat in the oceans.

Hysteresis

More generally, most forms of internal variability in the climate system can be recognized as a form of hysteresis, where the current state of climate does not immediately reflect the inputs. Because the Earth's climate system is so large, it moves slowly and has time-lags in its reaction to inputs. For example, a year of dry conditions may do no more than to cause lakes to shrink slightly or plains to dry marginally. In the following year however, these conditions may result in less rainfall, possibly leading to a drier year the next. When a critical point is reached after "x" number of years, the entire system may be altered inexorably. In this case, resulting in no rainfall at all. It is this hysteresis that has been mooted to be the possible progenitor of rapid and irreversible climate change

Effects of CO_2 on Climate Change

Increased carbon dioxide levels are thought to exacerbate the heating effects of the Greenhouse Effect by reducing the re-radiation of heat from the sun and, therefore, increasing the temperature contained in the atmosphere. As the ability of the atmosphere to capture and recycle energy emitted by the Earth's surface is essential to a stable climate, this heightened temperature may introduce a de-stabilising influence and potentially affect global weather patterns and, eventually, long-term climate change.

Other Factors Driving Climate Change

Plate Tectonics

On the longest time scales, plate tectonics will reposition continents, shape oceans, build and tear down mountains and generally serve to define the stage upon which climate exists. During the Carboniferous period, plate tectonics may have triggered the large-scale storage of Carbon and increased glaciation. More recently, plate motions have been implicated in the intensification of the present ice age when, approximately 3 million years ago, the North and South American plates collided to form the Isthmus of Panama and shut off direct mixing between the Atlantic and Pacific Oceans.

Solar Variation

The sun is the source of a large percentage of the heat energy input to the climate system. Lesser amounts of energy is provided by the gravitational pull of the Moon (manifested as tidal power), and geothermal energy. The energy output of the sun, which is converted to heat at the Earth's surface, is an integral part of the Earth's climate. Early in Earth's history, according to one theory, the sun was too cold to support liquid water at the Earth's surface, leading to what is known as the Faint young sun paradox Over the coming millenia, the sun will continue to brighten and produce a correspondingly higher energy output; as it continues through what is known as its "main sequence", and the Earth's atmosphere will be affected accordingly.

On more contemporary time scales, there are also a variety of forms of solar variation, including the 11-year solar cycle and longer-term modulations. However, the 11-year sunspot cycle does not appear to manifest itself clearly in the climatological data. Solar intensity variations are considered to have been influential in triggering the Little Ice Age, and for some of the warming observed from 1900 to 1950. The cyclical nature of the sun's energy output is not yet fully understood; it differs from the very slow change that is happening within the sun as it ages and evolves, with some studies pointing toward solar radiation increases from cyclical sunspot activity affecting Global Warming.

Orbital Variations

In their effect on climate, orbital variations are in some sense an extension of solar variability, because slight variations in the Earth's orbit lead to changes in the distribution and abundance of sunlight reaching the Earth's surface. These orbital variations, known as Milankovitch cycles, directly affect glacial activity. Eccentricity, axial tilt, and precession comprise the three dominant cycles that make up the variations in Earth's orbit. The combined effect of the variations in these three cycles creates changes in the seasonal reception of solar radiation on the Earth's surface. As such, Milankovitch Cycles affecting the increase or decrease of received solar radiation directly influence the Earth's climate system, and influence the advance and retreat of Earth's glaciers. Subtler variations are also present, such as the repeated advance and retreat of the Sahara desert in response to orbital precession

Volcanism

Volcanism is the process of conveying material from the depths of the Earth to the surface, as part of the process by which the planet removes excess heat and pressure from its interior. Volcanic eruptions, geysers and hot springs are all part of the volcanic process and all release varying levels of particulates into the atmosphere.

A single eruption of the kind that occurs several times per century can affect climate, causing cooling for a period of a few years or more. The eruption of Mount Pinatubo in 1991, for example, produced the second largest terrestrial eruption of the 20th century (after the 1912 eruption of Novarupta)and affected the climate substantially, with global temperatures dropping by about 0.5 °C (0.9 °F), and ozone depletion being temporarily substantially increased. Much larger eruptions, known as large igneous provinces, occur only a few times every hundred million years, but can reshape climate for millions of years and cause mass extinctions. Initially, it was thought that the dust ejected into the atmosphere from large volcanic eruptions was responsible for longer-term cooling by partially blocking the transmission of solar radiation to the Earth's surface. However, measurements indicate that most of the dust hurled into the atmosphere may return to the Earth's surface within as little as six months, given the right conditions.

Volcanoes are also part of the extended carbon cycle. Over very long (geological) time periods, they release carbon dioxide from the earth's interior, counteracting the uptake by sedimentary rocks and other geological carbon dioxide sinks. According to the US Geological Survey, however, estimates are that human activities generate more than 130 times the amount of carbon dioxide emitted by volcanoes.

Human Influences

Anthropogenic factors are human activities that change the environment. In some cases the chain of causality of human influence on the climate is direct and unambiguous (for example, the effects of irrigation on local humidity), whilst in other instances it is less clear. Various hypotheses for human-induced climate change have been argued for many years though, generally, the scientific debate has moved on from scepticism to a scientific consensus on climate change that human activity is the probable cause for the rapid changes in world climate in the past several decades. Consequently, the debate has largely shifted onto ways to reduce further human impact and to find ways to adapt to change that has already occurred.

Of most concern in these anthropogenic factors is the increase in CO_2 levels due to emissions from fossil fuel combustion, followed by aerosols (particulate matter in the atmosphere) and cement manufacture. Other factors, including land use, ozone depletion, animal agriculture and deforestation, are also of concern in the roles they play - both separately and in conjunction with other factors - in affecting climate.

Fossil Fuels

Carbon dioxide levels are substantially higher now than at any time in the last 750,000 years Beginning with the industrial revolution in the 19th Century and accelerating since, the human consumption of fossil fuels has elevated CO_2 levels from a concentration of approximately 280 ppm in pre-industrial times to around 387 ppm today The concentrations are increasing at a rate of about 2-3 ppm/year. If current rates of emission continue, these increasing concentrations are projected to reach a range of between 535 to 983 ppm by the end of the 21st century Along with rising methane levels, it is suggested that these changes may possibly cause an increase of 1.4-5.6°C between 1990 and 2100 (see global warming). Proposals by some scientists and international coalitions, aimed at attempting to prevent drastic climate change, have suggested setting goals to try to limit concentrations to 450 or 500 ppm.

Aerosols

Anthropogenic aerosols, particularly sulphate aerosols from fossil fuel combustion, exert a cooling influence. This, together with natural variability (such as Orbital Precession), may account for the relative "plateau" in the temperature of the middle part of the 20th-century

Cement Manufacture

Cement manufacture contributes CO_2 to the atmosphere when calcium carbonate is heated, producing lime and carbon dioxide, and also as a result of burning fossil fuels in the process. It is estimated that the cement industry produces around 5% of global man-made CO_2 emissions, of which 50%

is produced from the chemical process itself, and 40% from burning fuel to power that process. The amount of CO_2 emitted by the cement industry is more than 900 kg of CO_2 for every 1000 kg of cement produced.

Land-use

Prior to widespread fossil fuel use, humanity's largest effect on local climate was land use; irrigation, deforestation, and agriculture - on large scales - may fundamentally change the environment. For example, through the redirection of natural water courses or the destruction of animal habitats. Land use may also alter the local albedo by reducing ground cover and, therefore, altering the way sunlight is absorbed or reflected. There is evidence to suggest that the climate of Greece and other Mediterranean countries was permanently changed by widespread deforestation between 700 BC and 1 AD (the wood being used for shipbuilding, construction and fuel), with the result that the modern climate in the region is significantly hotter and drier, and the species of trees that were used for shipbuilding in the ancient world can no longer be found in the area. Similarly, large tracts of land in Australia were permanently altered shortly after humans arrived some 40,000+ years ago when vast areas of temperate rainforest were burned down to produce grasslands that favoured game that the new inhabitants preferred to eat. In more modern times, an assessment of conterminous U.S. biomass burning speculated that the approximate 8 fold reduction in Wildland Fire Emissions (aerosols) from the pre-industrial era to present caused by land use changes and land management decisions may have had a regional warming affect if not for fossil fuel burning emission increases occurring concurrently.

A controversial hypothesis by William Ruddiman - the early anthropocene hypothesis suggests that the rise of agriculture and its accompanying deforestation may have led to significant increases in carbon dioxide and methane levels during the period 5000-8000 years ago. These increases, which apparently reversed previous declines, may have been responsible for delaying the onset of the next Ice Age.

The 2007 Jet Propulsion Laboratory study found that the average mean temperature of California has risen approximately 2 degrees over the past 50 years. The change has been attributed mostly to extensive human development of the landscape.

Livestock

According to a 2006 United Nations report, Livestock's Long Shadow, livestock is responsible for some 18% of the world's greenhouse gas emissions as measured in CO_2 equivalents (this, however, also includes the net effect of deforestation in order to create grazing land, as well as livestock natural methane gas emissions), as well as 65% of human-induced nitrous oxide (which has 296 times the global warming potential of CO_2) and 37% of all human-induced methane (which has 23 times the global warming potential of CO_2). In the Amazon Rainforest, 70% of deforestation is specifically carried out to make way for grazing land, and so is a major factor in the 2006 UN FAO report; the first agricultural report to factor in land usage change and radiative forcing in regard to the influence of livestock production.

Interplay of Factors

However, a number of important positive feedback mechanisms do exist; the glacial and interglacial cycles of the recent epoch being an important example. It is mooted that orbital variations directly influence the timing for the retreat of ice sheets in proportion to the radiant heat (or insolation) arriving on the Earth's surface. However, as the ice sheets themselves reflect sunlight back into space the increased insolation may actually result in a cooling effect and the growth in the ice through what is known as the albedo feedback effect. Similarly, falling sea levels and expanding ice may decrease plant growth and indirectly lead to declines in carbon dioxide and methane, which may then lead to further cooling. Conversely, rising temperatures caused, for example, by anthropogenic emissions of greenhouse gases could lead to decreased snow and ice cover, revealing darker ground underneath and, consequently, result in more absorption of sunlight and a retreat of glacial ice. Either way, it is feared that these changes may overload the system sufficiently to produce the runaway feedback described and lead to sudden and disastrous climate change.

Water vapour, methane, and carbon dioxide can also act as significant influences on positive feedback, with their levels rising in response to a warming trend and, as a result, possibly accelerating that trend. Water vapor acts strictly as a feedback mechanism (excepting small amounts in the stratosphere), unlike the other major greenhouse gases, which may also act as forcings. More complex climate feedback influences include heat movement from the equatorial regions to the northern latitudes and involve the possibility of altered water currents with in the oceans or air currents within the atmosphere. A significant concern is that melting glacial ice from Greenland may interfere with (and possibly change) the thermohaline circulation of water in the North Atlantic, affecting the Gulf Stream that conveys warmer water in to replace sinking colder water. Alterations in these flows may affect the distribution of heat to the coast of Europe and the east coast of the United States, with a possible resulting change in climate.

Monitoring the Current Status of Climate

Testing for spatial dependence between independently measured value in an ordered set is based on applying Fisher's F-test to the ariance of a set and the first variance term of the ordered set. Carting statistically significant variance terms gives a sampling variogram that shows where spatial dependence in our sample space of time dissipates into randomness. The lag of a sampling varate statistic.

Scientsts use "Indicator time series" that represent the many aspects f climate and ecosystem status. The time history provides a histoical context. Current status of the climate is also monitored with climate indices.

Physical Evidence for Climatic Change

Evidnce for climatic change is taken from a variety of sources that an be used to reconstruct past climates. Most of the evidenc is indirect—climatic changes are inferred from changes in indicators that reflect climate, such as vegetation, ice cores dendrochronology, sea level change, and glacial geology.

A change in the type, distribution and coverage of vegetation may occur given a change in the climate; this much is obvious. However, to what extent particular plant life changes, dies or thrives, depends largely on the model of prediction used. In any given scenario, a mild change in climate may result in increased precipitation and warmth, resulting in improved plant growth and the subsequent sequestration of airborne CO_2. Larger, faster or more radical changes, however, may well result in vegetation stress, rapid plant loss and desertification in certain circumstances.

Ice Cores

Analysis of ice in a core drilled from a permafrost area, such as the Antarctic, can be used to show a link between temperature and global sea level variations. The air trapped in bubbles in the ice can also reveal the CO_2 variations of the atmosphere from the distant past, well before modern environmental influences. The study of these ice cores has been a significant indicator of the changes in CO_2 over many millennia, and continue to provide valuable information about the differences between ancient and modern atmospheric conditions.

Dendrochronology

Basically, Dendochronology is the analysis of tree ring growth patterns to determine the age of a tree. From a climate change viewpoint, however, Dendochronology can also indicate the climatic conditions for a given number of years. Wide and thick rings indicate a fertile, well-watered growing period, whilst thin, narrow rings indicate a time of lower rainfall and less-than-ideal growing conditions.

Pollen Analysis

Palynology is the science that studies contemporary and fossil palynomorphs, including pollen. Palynology is used to infer the geographical distribution of plant species, which vary under different climate conditions. Different groups of plants have pollen with distinctive shapes and surface textures, and since the outer surface of pollen is composed of a very resilient material, they resist decay. Changes in the type of pollen found in different sedimentation levels in lakes, bogs or river deltas indicate changes in plant communities; which are dependent on climate condition.

Insects

Remains of beetles are common in freshwater and land sediments. Different species of beetles tend to be found under different climatic conditions. Given the extensive lineage of beetles whose genetic makeup has not altered significantly over the millenia, knowledge of the present climatic range of the different species, and the age of the sediments in which remains are found, past climatic conditions may be inferred.

Current Sea Level Rise

Climate models for the substantiation of theories regarding global warming rely heavily on the measurement of long-term changes in global average sea level. Global sea level change for much of the last century has generally been estimated using tide gauge measurements collated over long periods of time to give a long-term average. More recently, altimeter measurements – in combination with accurately determined satellite orbits – have provided an improved measurement of global sea level change.

Advancing glaciers leave behind moraines that contain a wealth of material - including organic matter that may be accurately dated - recording the periods in which a glacier advanced and retreated. Similarly, by tephrochronological techniques, the lack of glacier cover can be identified by the presence of soil or volcanic tephra horizons whose date of deposit may also be precisely ascertained. Glaciers are considered one of the most sensitive climate indicators by the IPCC, and their recent observed variations are considered a prominent indicator of impending climate change. See also Retreat of glaciers since 1850.

The life cycles of many wild plants and animals are closely linked to the passing of the seasons; climatic changes can lead to interdependent pairs of species (for example, a wild flower and its pollinating insect) losing synchronization, if, for example, one has a cycle dependent on day length and the other on temperature or precipitation. In principle, at least, this could lead to extinctions or changes in the distribution and abundance of species. One phenomenon is the movement of species northwards in Europe. A recent study by Butterfly Conservation in the UK has shown that relatively common species with a southerly distribution have moved north, whilst scarce upland species have become rarer and lost territory towards the south. This picture has been mirrored across several invertebrate groups. Drier summers could lead to more periods of drought potentially affecting many species of animal and plant. For example, in the UK during the drought year of 2006 significant numbers of trees died or showed dieback on light sandy soils. In Australia, a study of scientific literature covering the recording of mass death occurrences of flying foxes in the Eastern states from 1994 has shown that tens of thousands of flying foxes (Pteropus) have died as a direct result of extreme heat events Wetter, milder winters might affect temperate mammals or insects by preventing them hibernating or entering torpor during periods when food is scarce. One predicted change is the ascendancy of 'weedy' or opportunistic species at the expense of scarcer species with narrower or more specialized ecological requirements. One example could be the expanses of bluebell seen in many woodlands in the UK. These have an early growing and flowering season before competing weeds can develop and the tree canopy closes. Milder winters can allow weeds to overwinter as adult plants or germinate sooner, whilst trees leaf earlier, reducing the length of the window for bluebells to complete their life cycle. Organisations such as Wildlife Trust, World Wide Fund for Nature, Birdlife International and the Audubon Society are actively monitoring and research the effects of climate change on biodiversity and advance policies in areas such as landscape scale conservation to promote adaptation to climate change.

GEOENGINEERING

Various techniques have been suggested to try to favorably change or maintain the climate. These include:

- *Solar radiation management by Albedo modification* - increasing the amount of sunlight reflected into space. Techniques range from the very large and technically complex, such as the space sunshade, to creating stratospheric sulfur aerosols or even simply painting large areas of roofing and paving materials white.
- *Greenhouse gas remediation, usually by carbon sequestration* - techniques such as biomass energy with carbon capture and storage, using lasers to break up CFCs in the atmosphere and iron fertilisation of oceans to stimulate phytoplankton growth.
- *Arctic or hydrological geoengineering* - typically seeking to preserve sea ice or adjust thermohaline circulation by using methods such as diverting rivers to keep warm water away from sea ice, or tethering icebergs to prevent them drifting into warmer waters and melting.

GREENHOUSE GAS

Greenhouse gases are gases in an atmosphere that absorb and emit radiation within the thermal infrared range. This process is the fundamental cause of the greenhouse effect.

In our solar system, the atmospheres of Venus, Mars and Titan also contain gases that cause greenhouse effects.

Greenhouse gases, mainly water vapor, are essential to helping determine the temperature of the Earth; without them this planet would likely be so cold as to be uninhabitable. Although many factors such as the sun and the water cycle are responsible for the Earth's weather and energy balance, if all else was held equal and stable, the planet's average temperature should be considerably lower without greenhouse gases.

Human activities have an impact upon the levels of greenhouse gases in the atmosphere, which has other effects upon the system, with their own possible repercussions. The most recent assessment report compiled by the IPCC observed that "changes in atmospheric concentrations of greenhouse gases and aerosols, land cover and solar radiation alter the energy balance of the climate system", and concluded that "increases in anthropogenic greenhouse gas concentrations is very likely to have caused most of the increases in global average temperatures since the mid-20th century".

Greenhouse Gases in Earth's Atmosphere

Earth's most abundant greenhouse gases are:

- water vapour
- carbon dioxide
- methane
- nitrous oxide
- ozone.

CFCs

When these gases are ranked by their contribution to the greenhouse effect, the most important are:

- water vapour, which contributes 36-70%
- carbon dioxide, which contributes 9-26%
- methane, which contributes 4-9%
- ozone, which contributes 3-7%.

The contribution to the greenhouse effect by a gas is affected by both the characteristics of the gas and its abundance. For example, on a molecule-for-molecule basis methane is a much stronger greenhouse gas than carbon dioxide, but it is present in much smaller concentrations so that its total contribution is smaller.

It is not possible to state that a certain gas causes an exact percentage of the greenhouse effect, because the influences of the various gases are not additive. The higher ends of the ranges quoted are for the gas alone; the lower ends, for the gas counting overlaps Other greenhouse gases include sulfur hexafluoride, hydrofluorocarbons and perfluorocarbons. See IPCC list of greenhouse gases. Some greenhouse gases are not often listed. For example, nitrogen trifluoride has a high global warming potential (GWP) but is only present in very small quantities.

Although contributing to many other physical and chemical reactions, the major atmospheric constituents, nitrogen (N_2), oxygen (O_2), and argon (Ar), are not greenhouse gases. This is because homonuclear diatomic molecules such as N_2 and O_2 and monatomic molecules such as Ar have no net change in their dipole moment when they vibrate and hence are almost totally unaffected by infrared light. Although heteronuclear diatomics such as carbon monoxide (CO) or hydrogen chloride (HCl) absorb IR, these molecules are short-lived in the atmosphere owing to their reactivity and solubility. As a consequence they do not contribute significantly to the greenhouse effect and are not often included when discussing greenhouse gases.

Late 19th century scientists experimentally discovered that N_2 and O_2 did not absorb infrared radiation (called, at that time, "dark radiation") and that water as a vapour and in cloud form, CO_2 and many other gases did absorb such radiation. It was recognized in the early 20th century that the greenhouse gases in the atmosphere caused the Earth's overall temperature to be higher than it would be without them.

Natural and Anthropogenic

Ice cores provide evidence for variation in greenhouse gas concentrations over the past 800,000 years. Both CO_2 and CH_4 vary between glacial and interglacial phases, and concentrations of these gases correlate strongly with temperature. Before the ice core record, direct data does not exist. However, various proxies and modelling suggests large variations; 500 Myr ago CO_2 levels were likely 10 times higher than now Indeed higher CO_2 concentrations are thought to have prevailed throughout most of the Phanerozoic eon, with concentrations four to six times current concentrations during the Mesozoic era, and ten to fifteen times current concentrations during the early Palaeozoic era until the middle of the Devonian period, about 400 Mya. The spread of land plants is thought to have reduced CO_2 concentrations during the late Devonian, and plant activities as both sources and sinks of CO_2 have since been important in providing stabilising feedbacks. Earlier still, a 200-million year period of intermittent, widespread glaciation extending close to the equator (Snowball Earth) appears to have been ended suddenly, about 550 Mya, by a colossal volcanic outgassing which raised the CO_2 concentration of the atmosphere abruptly to 12%, about 350 times modern levels, causing extreme greenhouse conditions and carbonate deposition as limestone at the rate of about 1mm per day. This episode marked the close of the Precambrian eon, and was succeeded by the generally warmer conditions of the Phanerozoic, during which multicellular animal and plant life evolved. No volcanic carbon dioxide emission of comparable scale has occurred since. In the modern era, emissions to the atmosphere from volcanoes are only about 1% of emissions from human sources.

Anthropogenic Greenhouse Gases

The projected temperature increase for a range of greenhouse gas stabilization scenarios (the coloured bands). The black line in middle of the shaded area indicates 'best estimates'; the red and the blue lines the likely limits. From the work of IPCC AR4, 2007.

Besides other changes to the environment, since about 1750 human activity has increased the concentration of carbon dioxide and other greenhouse gases. Measured atmospheric concentrations of carbon dioxide are currently 100 ppmv higher than pre-industrial levels. Natural sources of carbon dioxide are more than 20 times greater than sources due to human activity, but over periods longer than a few years natural sources are closely balanced by natural sinks such as weathering of continental rocks and photosynthesis of carbon compounds by plants and marine plankton. As a result of this balance, the atmospheric concentration of carbon dioxide had remained between 260 and 280 parts per million for the 10,000 years between the end of the last glacial maximum and the start of the industrial era.

It is likely anthropogenic warming, such as that due to elevated greenhouse gas levels, has had a discernible influence on many physical and biological systems. Projected changes in several climate factors, including atmospheric carbon dixoide, are projected to impact various issues such as freshwater resources, industry, food and health.

The main sources of greenhouse gases due to human activity are:

- burning of fossil fuels and deforestation leading to higher carbon dioxide concentrations. Land use change (mainly deforestation in the tropics) account for up to one third of total anthropogenic CO_2 emissions;
- livestock enteric fermentation and manure management paddy rice farming, land use and wetland changes, pipeline losses, and covered vented landfill emissions leading to higher methane atmospheric concentrations. Many of the newer style fully vented septic systems that enhance and target the fermentation process also are sources of atmospheric methane;
- use of chlorofluorocarbons (CFCs) in refrigeration systems, and use of CFCs and halons in fire suppression systems and manufacturing processes;
- agricultural activities, including the use of fertilizers, that lead to higher nitrous oxide (N_2O) concentrations.

The seven sources of CO_2 from fossil fuel combustion are (with percentage contributions for 2000-2004).

1. Solid fuels (e.g. coal): 35%
2. Liquid fuels (e.g. gasoline): 36%
3. Gaseous fuels (e.g. natural gas): 20%
4. Flaring gas industrially and at wells: <1%
5. Cement production: 3%
6. Non-fuel hydrocarbons: <1%
7. The "international bunkers" of shipping and air transport not included in national inventories: 4%

The US EPA ranks the major greenhouse gas contributing end-user sectors in the following order: industrial, transportation, residential, commercial and agricultural Major sources of an individual's GHG include home heating and cooling, electricity consumption, and transportation. Corresponding conservation measures are improving home building insulation, compact fluorescent lamps and choosing energy-efficient vehicles.

Carbon dioxide, methane, nitrous oxide and three groups of fluorinated gases (sulfur hexafluoride, HFCs, and PFCs) are the major greenhouse gases and the subject of the Kyoto Protocol, which came into force in 2005

Although CFCs are greenhouse gases, they are regulated by the Montreal Protocol, which was motivated by CFCs' contribution to ozone depletion rather than by their contribution to global warming. Note that ozone depletion has only a minor role in greenhouse warming though the two processes often are confused in the media.

Nitrogen trifluoride (NF3) is used in the manufacture of microelectronics. It is a strong greenhouse gas, but presently its concentration is very low and it is not subject to greenhouse gas treaties.

Role of Water Vapour

Water vapour accounts for the largest percentage of the greenhouse effect, between 36% and 66% for water vapor alone, and between 66% and 85% when factoring in clouds. Water vapor concentrations fluctuate regionally, but human activity does not directly affect water vapor concentrations except at local scales, such as near irrigated fields.

The *Clausius-Clapeyron relation* establishes that air can hold more water vapor per unit volume when it warms. This and other basic principles indicate that any warming associated with the increased concentration of the other greenhouse gases also increases the concentration of water vapor as well.

In climate matters, when a warming trend results in effects that induce further warming, the process is referred to as a "positive feedback"; when the effects induce cooling, the process is referred to as a "negative feedback". Because water vapor is the primary greenhouse gas and because warm air can hold more water vapor than cooler air, the primary positive feedback involves water vapor.

This positive feedback does not result in runaway global warming because it is offset by negative feedback, which stabilizes average global temperatures. One primary negative feedback is the effect of temperature on emission of infrared radiation: as the temperature of a body increases, the emitted radiation increases with the fourth power of its absolute temperature.

Other important considerations involve water vapor being the only greenhouse gas whose concentration is highly variable in space and time in the atmosphere and the only one that also exists in both liquid and solid phases, frequently changing to and from each of the three phases or existing in mixes. Such considerations include clouds themselves, air and water vapor density interactions when they are the same or different temperatures, the absorption and release of kinetic energy as water evaporates and condenses to and from vapor, and behaviors related to vapor partial pressure. For example, the release of latent heat by rain in the ITCZ drives atmospheric circulation, clouds vary atmospheric albedo levels, and the oceans provide evaporative cooling that modulates the greenhouse effect down from estimated 67 °C surface temperature.

Greenhouse Gas Emissions

Measurements from *Antarctic ice cores* show that before industrial emissions started, atmospheric CO_2 levels were about 280 parts per million by volume (ppmv), and it appears that concentrations stayed between 260 and 280 during the preceding ten thousand years One study using evidence from stomata of fossilized leaves suggests greater variability, with carbon dioxide levels above 300 ppm during the period seven to ten thousand years ago though others have argued that these findings more likely reflect calibration or contamination problems rather than actual CO_2 variability. Because of the way air is trapped in ice (pores in the ice close off slowly to form bubbles deep within the firn) and the time period represented in each ice sample analyzed, these figures represent averages of atmospheric concentrations of up to a few centuries rather than annual or decadal levels.

Since the beginning of the Industrial Revolution, the concentrations of most of the greenhouse gases have increased. For example, the concentration of carbon dixode has increased by about 36% to 380 ppmv, or 100 ppmv over modern pre-industrial levels. The first 50 ppmv increase took place in about 200 years, from the start of the Industrial Revolution to around 1973; however the next 50 ppmv increase took place in about 33 years, from 1973 to 2006.

Data also shows the concentration is increasing at a higher rate. In the 1960s, the average annual increase was only 37% of what it was in 2000 through 2007.

The other greenhouse gases produced from human activity show similar increases in both amount and rate of increase. Many observations are available online in a variety of *Atmospheric Chemistry Observational Databases*.

Removal from the Atmosphere and Global Warming Potential

This section deals with natural processes. For projects to deliberately remove greenhouses gases from the atmosphere, see geoengineering, carbon dioxide scrubbing and greenhouse gas remediation.

Aside from water vapour, which has a residence time of about nine days, major greenhouse gases are well-mixed, and take many years to leave the atmosphere. Although it is not easy to know with precision how long it takes greenhouse gases to leave the atmosphere, there are estimates for the principal greenhouse gases.

Natural Processes

Greenhouse gases can be removed from the atmosphere by various processes:

- as a consequence of a physical change (condensation and precipitation remove water vapor from the atmosphere);
- as a consequence of chemical reactions within the atmosphere. This is the case for methane. It is oxidized by reaction with naturally occurring hydroxyl radical, OH and degraded to CO_2 and water vapor at the end of a chain of reactions (the contribution of the CO_2 from the oxidation of methane is not included in the methane Global warming potential). This also includes solution and solid phase chemistry occurring in atmospheric aerosols;
- as a consequence of a physical interchange at the interface between the atmosphere and the other compartments of the planet. An example is the mixing of atmospheric gases into the oceans at the boundary layer;
- as a consequence of a chemical change at the interface between the atmosphere and the other compartments of the planet. This is the case for CO_2, which is reduced by photosynthesis of plants, and which, after dissolving in the oceans, reacts to form carbonic acid and bicarbonate and carbonate ions;
- as a consequence of a *photochemical change*. Halocarbons are dissociated by UV light releasing Cl and F as free radicals in the stratosphere with harmful effects on ozone (halocarbons are generally too stable to disappear by chemical reaction in the atmosphere).

Atmospheric Lifetime

Jacob defines the lifetime t of an atmospheric species X in a one-box model as the average time that a molecule of X remains in the box. Mathematically t can be defined as the ratio of the mass m (in kg) of X in the box to its removal rate, which is the sum of the flow of X out of the box (Fout), chemical loss of X (L), and deposition of X (D) (all in kg/sec):

$$\tau = \frac{m}{F_{out} + L + D}$$

The atmospheric lifetime of a species therefore measures the time required to restore equilibrium following an increase in its concentration in the atmosphere. Individual atoms or molecules may be lost or deposited to sinks such as the soil, the oceans and other waters, or vegetation and other biological systems, reducing the excess to background concentrations. The average time taken to achieve this is the mean lifetime. The atmospheric lifetime of CO_2 is often incorrectly stated to be only a few years because that is the average time for any CO_2 molecule to stay in the atmosphere before being removed by mixing into the ocean, photosynthesis, or other processes. However, this ignores the balancing fluxes of CO_2 into the atmosphere from the other reservoirs. It is the net concentration changes of the various greenhouse gases by all sources and sinks that determines atmospheric lifetime, not just the removal processes.

Global Warming Potential

The global warming potential (GWP) depends on both the efficiency of the molecule as a greenhouse gas and its atmospheric lifetime. GWP is measured relative to the same mass of CO_2 and evaluated for a specific timescale. Thus, if a molecule has a high GWP on a short time scale (say 20 years) but has only a short lifetime, it will have a large GWP on a 20 year scale but a small one on a 100 year scale. Conversely, if a molecule has a longer atmospheric lifetime than CO2 its GWP will increase with time.

Examples of the atmospheric lifetime and GWP for several greenhouse gases include:

- *Carbon dioxide* has a variable atmospheric lifetime, and cannot be specified precisely. Recent work indicates that recovery from a large input of atmospheric CO_2 from burning fossil fuels will result in an effective lifetime of tens of thousands of years. Carbon dioxide is defined to have a GWP of 1 over all time periods.
- *Methane* has an atmospheric lifetime of 12 ± 3 years and a GWP of 72 over 20 years, 25 over 100 years and 7.6 over 500 years. The decrease in GWP at longer times is because methane is degraded to water and CO_2 through chemical reactions in the atmosphere.
- *Nitrous oxide* has an atmospheric lifetime of 114 years and a GWP of 289 over 20 years, 298 over 100 years and 153 over 500 years.
- *CFC-12* has an atmospheric lifetime of 100 years and a GWP of 11000 over 20 years, 10900 over 100 years and 5200 over 500 years.
- *HCFC-22* has an atmospheric lifetime of 12 years and a GWP of 5160 over 20 years, 1810 over 100 years and 549 over 500 years.
- *Tetrafluoromethane* has an atmospheric lifetime of 50,000 years and a GWP of 5210 over 20 years, 7390 over 100 years and 11200 over 500 years.
- *Sulphur hexafluoride* has an atmospheric lifetime of 3,200 years and a GWP of 16300 over 20 years, 22800 over 100 years and 32600 over 500 years.
- *Nitrogen trifluoride* has an atmospheric lifetime of 740 years and a GWP of 12300 over 20 years, 17200 over 100 years and 20700 over 500 years.

The use of *CFC-12* (except some essential uses) has been phased out due to its ozone depleting properties. The phasing-out of less active *HCFC-compounds* will be completed in 2030.

Airborne Fraction

Airborne fraction (AF) is the proportion of a emission (e.g. CO_2) remaining in the atmosphere after a specified time. Canadell (2007) define the annual AF as the ratio of the atmospheric CO_2 increase in a given year to that year's total emissions, and calculate that of the average 9.1 PgC y^{-1} of total anthropogenic emissions from 2000 to 2006, the AF was 0.45. For CO_2 the AF over the last 50 years (1956-2006) has been increasing at 0.25 ± 0.21%/year.

Related Effects

Carbon monoxide has an indirect radiative effect by elevating concentrations of methane and tropospheric ozone through scavenging of atmospheric constituents (e.g., the hydroxyl radical, OH) that would otherwise destroy them. Carbon monoxide is created when carbon-containing fuels are burned incompletely. Through natural processes in the atmosphere, it is eventually oxidized to carbon dioxide. Carbon monoxide has an atmospheric lifetime of only a few months and as a consequence is spatially more variable than longer-lived gases.

Another potentially important indirect effect comes from methane, which in addition to its direct radiative impact also contributes to ozone formation. Shindell et al (2005) argue that the contribution to climate change from methane is at least double previous estimates as a result of this effect.

8

CHEMICAL ELEMENT

A chemical element is a type of atom that is distinguished by its atomic number; that is, by the number of protons in its nucleus. The term is also used to refer to a pure chemical substance composed of atoms with the same number of protons. Common examples of elements are iron, copper, silver, gold, hydrogen, carbon, nitrogen, and oxygen. In total, 117 elements have been observed as of 2008, of which 92 occur naturally on Earth. 80 elements have stable isotopes (namely all elements with atomic numbers 1 to 82, except elements 43 and 61 (technetium and promethium). Elements with atomic numbers 83 or higher (bismuth and above) are inherently unstable, and undergo radioactive decay. The elements from atomic number 83 to 94 have no stable nuclei, but are nevertheless found in nature, either surviving as remnants of the primordial stellar nucleosynthesis which produced the elements in the solar system, or else produced as short-lived daughter-isotopes through the natural decay of uranium and thorium.

All chemical matter consists of these elements. New elements of higher atomic number are discovered from time to time, as products of artificial nuclear reactions.

History

Several old philosophies used a set of archetypal classical elements to explain patterns in nature. The term 'element' was originally used to refer to a state of matter (solid/earth, liquid/water, gas/air, and plasma/fire) or a phase of matter (as in the Chinese *Wu Xing*), rather than the chemical elements of modern science. The Greek, Indian (*Tattva* and *Mahabhuta*) and Japanese (*go dai*) traditions essentially had the same five elements: Air, Earth, Fire, Water and Aether.

The term 'elements' (*stoicheia*) was first used by the Greek philosopher Plato in about 360 BCE, in his dialogue Timaeus, which includes a discussion of the composition of inorganic and organic bodies and is a rudimentary treatise on chemistry. Plato assumed that the minute particle of each element corresponded to one of the regular polyhedra: tetrahedron (fire), octahedron (air), icosahedron (water), and cube (earth).

Adding to the four elements of the Greek philosopher Empedocles, in about 350 BC, Aristotle also used the term "element"and conceived of a fifth element called "quintessence", which formed the heavens. Aristotle defined an element as:

Element – one of those bodies into which other bodies can be decomposed and which itself is not capable of being divided into other.

Building on the theory in circa 790, Arab/Persian chemist and alchemist, Jabir ibn Hayyan (Geber), postulated that metals were formed out of two elements: sulphur, 'the stone which burns', which characterized the principle of combustibility, and mercury, which contained the idealized principle of metallic properties Shortly thereafter, this evolved into the Arabic concept of the three principles: sulphur giving flammability or combustion, mercury giving volatility and stability, and salt giving solidity.

In the 10th century, Persian physician and alchemist Muhammad ibn Zakariya Razi (Rhazes) wrote the Doubts concerning Galen, in which he refuted both the Galenic medical theory of four humours and the underlying ancient concept of four classical elements. He carried out an experiment which would upset these theories by inserting a liquid with a different temperature into a body resulting in an increase or decrease of bodily heat, which resembled the temperature of that particular fluid. Razi noted particularly that a warm drink would heat up the body to a degree much higher than its own natural temperature, thus the drink would trigger a response from the body, rather than transferring only its own warmth or coldness to it. Razi's chemical experiments suggested other qualities of matter, such as "oiliness" and "sulfurousness", or inflammability and salinity, which were not readily explained by the traditional fire, water, earth and air division of elements.

In 1524, Swiss chemist Paracelsus adopted Aristotle's four element theory, but reasoned that they appeared in bodies as Geber's three principles. Paracelsus saw these principles as fundamental, and justified them by recourse to the description of how wood burns in fire. Mercury included the cohesive principle, so that when it left in smoke the wood fell apart. Smoke represented the volatility (the mercury principle), the heat-giving flames represented flammability (sulphur), and the remnant ash represented solidity (salt).

In 1669, German physician and chemist Johann Becher published his Physica Subterranea. In modification on the ideas of Paracelsus, he argued that the constituents of bodies are air, water, and three types of earth: terra fluida, the mercurial element, which contributes fluidity and volatility; terra lapida, the solidifying element, which produces fusibility or the binding quality; and terra pinguis, the fatty element, which gives material substance its oily and combustible qualities These three earths correspond with Geber's three principles. A piece of wood, for example, according to Becher, is composed of ash and terra pinguis; when the wood is burnt, the terra pinguis is released, leaving the ash. In other words, in combustion the fatty earth burns away.

In 1661, Robert Boyle showed that there were more than just four classical elements as the ancients had assumed. The first modern list of chemical elements was given in Antoine Lavoisier's 1789 Elements of Chemistry, which contained thirty-three elements, including light and caloric. By 1818, Jöns Jakob Berzelius had determined atomic weights for forty-five of the forty-nine accepted elements. Dmitri Mendeleev had sixty-six elements in his periodic table of 1869.

From Boyle until the early 20th century, an element was defined as a pure substance that cannot be decomposed into any simpler substance. Put another way, a chemical element cannot be transformed into other chemical elements by chemical processes. In 1913, Henry Moseley discovered that the physical basis of the atomic number of the atom was its nuclear charge, which eventually led to the current definition. The current definition also avoids some ambiguities due to isotopes and allotropes.

By 1919, there were seventy-two known elements In 1955, element 101 was discovered and named mendelevium in honor of Mendeleev, the first to arrange the elements in a periodic manner. In October 2006, the synthesis of element 118 was reported; however, element 117 has not yet been created in the laboratory.

Description

The lightest elements are hydrogen and helium, both theoretically created by Big Bang nucleosynthesis during the first 20 minutes of the universe in a ratio of around 3:1 by mass (approximately 12:1 by number of atoms). Almost all other elements found in nature, including some further hydrogen and helium created since then, were made by various natural or (at times) artificial methods of nucleosynthesis, including occasionally breakdown activities such as nuclear fission, alpha decay, cluster decay, and cosmic ray spallation.

As of 2006, there are 117 known elements (in this context, "known" means observed well enough, even from just a few decay products, to have been differentiated from any other element) Of these 117 elements, 94 occur naturally on Earth. Six of these occur in extreme trace quantities: technetium, atomic number 43; promethium, number 61; astatine, number 85; francium, number 87; neptunium, number 93; and plutonium, number 94. These 94 elements, and also possibly element 98 californium, have been detected in the universe at large, in the spectra of stars and also supernovae, where short-lived radioactive elements are newly being made.

The remaining 22 elements not found on Earth or in astronomical spectra have been derived artificially. All of the elements that are derived solely through artificial means are radioactive with very short half-lives; if any atoms of these elements were present at the formation of Earth, they are extremely likely to have already decayed, and if present in novae, have been in quantities too small to have been noted. Technetium was the first purportedly non-naturally occurring element to be synthesized, in 1937, although trace amounts of technetium have since been found in nature, and the element may have been discovered naturally in 1925. This pattern of artificial production and later natural discovery has been repeated with several other radioactive naturally occurring trace elements.

Lists of the elements are available by name, by symbol, by atomic number, by density, by melting point, and by boiling point as well as Ionization energies of the elements. The most convenient presentation of the elements is in the periodic table, which groups elements with similar chemical properties together.

Atomic Number

The atomic number of an element, Z, is equal to the number of protons which defines the element. For example, all carbon atoms contain 6 protons in their nucleus; so the atomic number "Z" of carbon is 6. Carbon atoms may have different numbers of neutrons, which are known as isotopes of the element.

The number of protons in the atomic nucleus also determines its electric charge, which in turn determines the electrons of the atom in its non-ionized state. This in turn (by means of the Pauli exclusion principle) determines the atom's various chemical properties. So all carbon atoms, for example, ultimately have identical chemical properties because they all have the same number of protons in their nucleus, and therefore have the same atomic number. It is for this reason that atomic number rather than mass number (or atomic weight) is considered the identifying characteristic of an element.

Atomic Mass

The mass number of an element, A, is the number of nucleons (protons and neutrons) in the atomic nucleus. Different isotopes of a given element are distinguished by their mass numbers, which are conventionally written as a super-index on the left hand side of the atomic symbol (e.g., ^{238}U).

The relative atomic mass of an element is the average of the atomic masses of all the chemical element's isotopes as found in a particular environment, weighted by isotopic abundance, relative to the atomic mass unit (u). This number may be a fraction which is not close to a whole number, due to the averaging process. On the other hand, the atomic mass of a pure isotope is quite close to its mass number. Whereas the mass number is a natural (or whole) number, the atomic mass of a single isotope is a real number which is close to a natural number. In general, it differs slightly from the mass number as the mass of the protons and neutrons is not exactly 1 u, the electrons also contribute slightly to the atomic mass, and because of the nuclear binding energy. For example, the mass of ^{19}F is 18.9984032 u. The only exception to the atomic mass of an isotope not being a natural number is ^{12}C, which has a mass of exactly 12, due to the definition of u (it is fixed as 1/12th of the mass of a free carbon-12 atom, exactly).

Isotopes

Isotopes are atoms of the same element (that is, with the same number of protons in their atomic nucleus), but having different numbers of neutrons. Most (66 of 94) naturally occurring elements have more than one stable isotope. Thus, for example, there are three main isotopes of carbon. All carbon atoms have 6 protons in the nucleus, but they can have either 6, 7, or 8 neutrons. Since the mass numbers of these are 12, 13 and 14 respectively, the three isotopes of carbon are known as carbon-12, carbon-13, and carbon-14, often abbreviated to ^{12}C, ^{13}C, and ^{14}C. Carbon in everyday life and in chemistry is a mixture of ^{12}C, ^{13}C, and ^{14}C atoms.

All three of the isotopes of carbon have the same chemical properties. But they have different nuclear properties. In this example, carbon-12 and carbon-13 are stable atoms, but carbon-14 is unstable; it is slightly radioactive, decaying over time into other elements.

Like carbon, some isotopes of various elements are radioactive and decay into other elements upon radiating an alpha or beta particle. For certain elements, all their isotopes are radioactive isotopes: specifically the elements without any stable isotopes are technetium (atomic number 43), promethium (atomic number 61), and all observed elements with atomic numbers greater than 82.

Of the 80 elements with a stable isotope, 26 have only one stable isotope, and the mean number of stable isotopes for the 80 stable elements is 3.1 stable isotopes per element. The largest number of stable isotopes that occur for an element is 10 (for tin, element 50).

Allotropes

Some elements can be found as multiple elementary substances, known as allotropes, which differ in their structure and properties. For example, carbon can be found as diamond, which has a tetrahedral structure around each carbon atom; graphite, which has layers of carbon atoms with a hexagonal structure stacked on top of each other, graphene, which is a single layer of graphite which is incredibly strong, fullerenes, which have nearly spherical shapes, and carbon nanotubes, which are tubes with a hexagonal structure – there are two types of nanotubes, conducting and semi-conducting. The ability for an element to exist in one of many structural forms is known as 'allotropy'.

Standard State

The standard state, or reference state, of an element is defined as its thermodynamically most stable state at 1 bar at a given temperature (typically at 298.15 K). In thermochemistry, an element is defined to have an enthalpy of formation of zero in its standard state. For example, the reference state for carbon is graphite, because it is more stable than the other allotropes.

Nomenclature

The naming of elements precedes the atomic theory of matter, although at the time it was not known which chemicals were elements and which compounds. When it was learned, existing names (e.g., gold, mercury, iron) were kept in most countries, and national differences emerged over the names of elements either for convenience, linguistic niceties, or nationalism. For example, the Germans use "Wasserstoff" for "hydrogen", "Sauerstoff" for "oxygen" and "Stickstoff" for "nitrogen", while English and some romance languages use "sodium" for "natrium" and "potassium" for "kalium", and the French, Italians, Greeks, Portuguese and Poles prefer "azote/ azot/azoto" for "nitrogen".

But for international trade, the official names of the chemical elements both ancient and recent are decided by the International Union of Pure and Applied Chemistry, which has decided on a sort of international English language. That organization has recently prescribed that "aluminium" and "caesium" take the place of the US spellings "aluminum" and "cesium", while the US "sulfur" takes the place of the British "sulphur". But chemicals which are practicable to be sold in bulk within many countries, however, still have national names, and those which do not use the Latin alphabet cannot be expected to use the IUPAC name. According to IUPAC, the full name of an element is not capitalized, even if it is derived from a proper noun such as the elements californium or einsteinium (unless it would be capitalized by some other rule). Isotopes of chemical elements are also uncapitalized if written out: carbon-12 or uranium-235.

In the second half of the twentieth century physics laboratories became able to produce nuclei of chemical elements that have a half life too short for them to remain in any appreciable amounts. These are also named by IUPAC, which generally adopts the name chosen by the discoverer. This can lead to the controversial question of which research group actually discovered an element, a question which delayed the naming of elements with atomic number of 104 and higher for a considerable time.

Precursors of such controversies involved the nationalistic namings of elements in the late nineteenth century. For example, lutetium was named in reference to Paris, France. The Germans were reluctant to relinquish naming rights to the French, often calling it cassiopeium. The British discoverer of niobium originally named it columbium, in reference to the New World. It was used extensively as such by American publications prior to international standardization.

Chemical Symbols	Name	Atomic number	Origin of Symbol
A	Argon	18	Current symbol is Ar
Ab	Alabamine	85	Discredited claim to discovery of astatine
Am	Alabamium	85	Discredited claim to discovery of astatine
An	Athenium	99	Proposed name for einsteinium
Ao	Ausonium	93	Discredited claim to discovery of neptunium
Az	Azote	7	Former name for nitrogen
Bv	Brevium	91	Former name for protactinium
Bz	Berzelium	59	Suggested name for praseodymium
Cb	Columbium	41	Former name of niobium
Cb	Columbium	95	Suggested name for americium
Cp	Cassiopeium	71	Former name for lutetium
Ct	Centurium	100	Proposed name for fermium
Ct	Celtium	72	Former name of hafnium
Da	Danubium	43	Suggested name for technetium
Db	Dubnium	104	Proposed name for rutherfordium. The symbol and name were used for element 105

(Contd...)

Chemical Symbols	Name	Atomic number	Origin of Symbol
Eb	Ekaboron	21	Name given by Mendeleev to an as of then undiscovered element. When discovered, scandium closely matched the prediction.
E1	Ekaaluminium	31	Name given by Mendeleev to an as of then undiscovered element. When discovered, gallium closely matched the prediction.
Em	Emanation	86	Also called radium emanation, the name was originally given by Friedrich Ernst Dorn in 1900. In 1923, this element officially became radon (the name given at one time to ^{222}Rn, an isotope identified in the decay chain of radium).
Em	Ekamangan	43	Name given by Mendeleev to an as of then undiscovered element. When discovered, technetium closely matched the prediction.
Es	Ekasilicon	32	Name given by Mendeleev to an as of then undiscovered element. When discovered, germanium closely matched the prediction.
Es	Esperium	94	Discredited claim to discovery of plutonium.
Fa	Francium	87	Current symbol is **Fr**.
Fr	Florentium	61	Discredited claim to discovery of promethium.

(Contd…)

Chemical Symbols	Name	Atomic number	Origin of Symbol
Gl	Glucinium	4	Former name of beryllium
Ha	Hahnium	105	Proposed name for dubnium
Ha	Hahnium	108	Proposed name for hassium.
Il	Illinium	61	Discredited claim to discovery of promethium
Jg	Jargonium	72	Discredited claim to discovery of hafnium.
Jo	Joliotium	105	Proposed name dubnium
Ku	Kurchatovium	104	Proposed name for rutherfordium
Lw	Lawrencium	103	Current symbol is **Lr**.
M	Muriaticum	17	Former name of chlorine
Ma	Masurium	43	Disputed claim to discovery of technetium
Md	Mendelevium	97	Proposed name for berkelium. The symbol and name were later used for element 101
Me	Mendelevium	68	Suggested name for erbium
Ms	Masrium	49	Discredited claim of discovery of indium
Mt	Meitnium	91	Suggested name for protactinium
Mv	Mendelevium	101	Current symbol is **Md**

(Contd…)

Chemical Symbols	Name	Atomic number	Origin of Symbol
Ng	Norwegium	72	Discredited claim to discovery of hafnium
Ni	Niton	86	Former name for radon
No	Norium	72	Discredited claim to discovery of hafnium
Ns	Nielsbohrium	105	Proposed name for dubnium
Ns	Nielsbohrium	107	Proposed name for bohrium
Nt	Niton	86	Suggested name for radon
Ny	Neoytterbium	70	Former name of ytterbium
Od	Odinium	62	Suggested name for samarium
Pc	Policium	110	Proposed name for darmstadtium
Pe	Pelopium	41	Former name for niobium
Po	Potassium	19	Current symbol is **K**
Rf	Rutherfordium	106	Proposed name for seaborgium. The symbol and name were instead used for element 104.
Sa	Samarium	62	Current symbol is **Sm**
So	Sodium	11	Current symbol is **Na**
Sp	Spectrium	70	Suggested name for ytterbium

(Contd…)

Chemical Symbols	Name	Atomic number	Origin of Symbol
St	Antimony	51	Current symbol is **Sb**
Tn	Tungsten	74	Current symbol is **W**
Tu	Thulium	69	Current symbol is **Tm**
Tu	Tungsten	74	Current symbol is **W**
Ty	Tyrium	60	Suggested name for neodymium
Unb	Unnilbium	102	Temperature name given to nobelium until it was permanently named by IUPAC.
Une	Unnilennium	109	Temporary name given to meitnerium until it was permanently named by IUPAC.
Unh	Unnilhexium	106	Temporary name given to seaborgium until it was permanently named by IUPAC.
Uno	Unniloctium	108	Temporary name given to hassium until it was permanently named by IUPAC.
Unp	Unnilpentium	105	Temporary name given to dubnium until it was permanently named by IUPAC
Unq	Unnilquadium	104	Temporary name given to rutherfordium until it was permanently named by IUPAC

(Contd...)

Chemical Symbols	Name	Atomic number	Origin of Symbol
Uns	Unnilseptium	107	Temporary name given to bohrium until it was permanently named by IUPAC.
Unt	Unniltrium	103	Temporary name given to lawrencium until it was permanently named by IUPAC.
Unu	Unnilunium	101	Temporary name given to mendelevium until it was permanently named by IUPAC.
Uun	Ununilium	110	Temporary name given to darmstadtium until it was permanently named by IUPAC.
Uuu	Unununium	111	Temporary name given to roentgenium until it was permanently named by IUPAC
Vi	Virginium	87	Discredited claim to discovery of francium
Vm	Virginium	87	Discredited claim to discovery of francium
Yt	Yttrium	39	Current symbol is **Y.**

Specific Chemical Elements

Before chemistry became a science, alchemists had designed arcane symbols for both metals and common compounds. These were however used as abbreviations in diagrams or procedures; there was no concept of atoms combining to form molecules. With his advances in the atomic theory of matter, John Dalton devised his own simpler symbols, based on circles, which were to be used to depict molecules.

The current system of chemical notation was invented by Berzelius. In this typographical system chemical symbols are not used as mere abbreviations - though each consists of letters of the Latin alphabet - they are symbols intended to be used by peoples of all languages and alphabets. The first of these symbols were intended to be fully universal; since Latin was the common language of science at that time, they were abbreviations based on the Latin names of metals - Fe comes from Ferrum, Ag from Argentum. The symbols were not followed by a period (full stop) as abbreviations were. Later chemical elements were also assigned unique chemical symbols, based on the name of the element, but not necessarily in English. For example, sodium has the chemical symbol 'Na' after the Latin natrium. The same applies to "W" (wolfram) for tungsten, "Hg" (hydrargyrum) for mercury, "K" (kalium) for potassium, "Au" (aurum) for gold, "Pb" (plumbum) for lead, and "Sb" (stibium) for antimony.

Chemical symbols are understood internationally when element names might need to be translated. There are sometimes differences; for example, the Germans have used "J" instead of "I" for iodine, so the character would not be confused with a roman numeral.

The first letter of a chemical symbol is always capitalized, as in the preceding examples, and the subsequent letters, if any, are always lower case (small letters).

General Chemical Symbols

There are also symbols for series of chemical elements, for comparative formulas. These are one capital letter in length, and the letters are reserved so they are not permitted to be given for the names of specific elements. For example, an "X" is used to indicate a variable group amongst a class of compounds (though usually a halogen), while "R" is used for a radical, meaning a compound structure such as a hydrocarbon chain. The letter "Q" is reserved for "heat" in a chemical reaction. "Y" is also often used as a general chemical symbol, although it is also the symbol of yttrium. "Z" is also frequently used as a general variable group. "L" is used to represent a general ligand in inorganic and organometallic chemistry. "M" is also often used in place of a general metal.

Isotope Symbols

The three main isotopes of the element hydrogen are often written as H for protium, D for deuterium and T for tritium. This is in order to make it easier to use them in chemical equations, as it replaces the need to write out the mass number for each atom. It is written like this:

D_2O (Heavy Water)

Instead of writing it like this:

^2H_2O

The Periodic Table

The periodic table of the chemical elements is a tabular method of displaying the chemical elements. Although precursors to this table exist, its invention is generally credited to Russian chemist Dmitri Mendeleev in 1869. Mendeleev intended the table to illustrate recurring ("periodic") trends in the properties of the elements. The layout of the table has been refined and extended over time, as new elements have been discovered, and new theoretical models have been developed to explain chemical behavior.

The periodic table is now ubiquitous within the academic discipline of chemistry, providing an extremely useful framework to classify, systematize and compare all the many different forms of chemical behavior. The table has also found wide application in physics, biology, engineering, and industry. The current standard table contains 117 confirmed elements as of January 27, 2008 (while element 118 has been synthesized, element 117 has not).

Recently Discovered Element Claims

The first transuranium element (element with atomic number greater than 92) discovered was neptunium in 1940. As of August 2007, only the elements up to 111, roentgenium, have been confirmed as valid by IUPAC, while more or less reliable claims have been made for synthesis of elements 112, 113, 114, 115, 116 and 118. The heaviest element that is believed to have been synthesized to date is element 118, ununoctium, on October 9, 2006, by the Flerov Laboratory of Nuclear Reactions in Dubna, Russia.

Element 117, ununseptium, has not yet been created or discovered, but its place in the periodic table is preestablished.

On April 24, 2008, Amnon Marinov and six other researchers, claimed that element 122 has been detected as a naturally occurring in a thorium deposit This is the first naturally occurring heavy element in more than 50 years. It has yet to be proved as it is still under confirmation by the university but could be a major development as previously all transuranic elements were artificial.

Abundance of the Chemical Elements

The abundance of a chemical element measures how relatively common the element is, or how much of the element there is by comparison to all other elements. Abundance may be variously measured by the mass-fraction (the same as weight fraction), or mole-fraction (fraction of atoms, or sometimes fraction of molecules, in gases), or by volume fraction. Measurement by volume-fraction is a common abundance measure in mixed gases such as atmospheres, which is close to molecular mole-fraction for ideal gas mixtures (i.e., gas mixtures at relatively low densities and pressures).

For example, the mass-fraction abundance of oxygen in water is about 89%, because that is the fraction of water's mass which is oxygen. However, the mole-fraction abundance of oxygen in water is only 33% because only 1 atom in 3 in water is an oxygen atom. In the universe as a whole, and in the atmospheres of gas-giant planets such as Jupiter, the mass-fraction abundances of hydrogen and helium are about 74% and 23-25% respectively, while the (atomic) mole-fractions of these elements are closer to 92% and 8%. However, since hydrogen is diatomic while helium is not in the conditions of Jupiter's outer atmosphere, the molecular mole-fraction (fraction of total gas molecules, or fraction of atmosphere by volume) of hydrogen in the outer atmosphere of Jupiter is about 86%, and for helium, 13%.

Most abundances in this article are given as mass-fraction abundances.

Abundance of Elements in the Universe

The elements - namely ordinary (baryonic) matter made out of protons and neutrons (as well as electrons) - are only a small part of the content of the Universe. Cosmological observations suggest that about 73% of the universe consists of dark energy, 23% is composed of dark matter and only 4% corresponds to the visible baryonic matter which constitutes stars, planets and living beings. Dark matter has not yet been detected in a particle physics detector, and the nature of the dark energy is not yet understood.

Solar System's most abundant isotopes		Isotope mass fraction in parts per million
Hydrogen	–	1 705,700
Helium	–	4 275,200
Oxygen	–	16 5,920
Carbon	–	12 3,032
Neon	–	20 1,548
Iron	–	56 1,169
Nitrogen	–	14 1,105
Silicon	–	28 653
Magnesium	–	24 513
Sulfur	–	32 396
Neon	–	22 208
Magnesium	–	26 79
Argon	–	36 77
Iron	–	54 72
Magnesium	–	25 69
Calcium	–	40 60
Aluminum	–	27 58
Nickel	–	58 49
Carbon	–	13 37
Helium	–	3 35
Silicon	–	29 34
Sodium	–	23 33
Iron	–	57 28
Hydrogen	–	2 23
Silicon	–	30 23

Hydrogen and helium are estimated to make up roughly 74% and 24% of all baryonic matter in the universe respectively. Despite comprising only a very small fraction of the universe, the remaining "heavy elements" can greatly influence astronomical phenomena. Only about 2% (by mass) of the Milky Way galaxy's disk is composed of heavy elements.

These other elements are generated by stellar processes. In astronomy, a "metal" is any element other than hydrogen or helium. This distinction is significant because hydrogen and helium (together with trace amounts of lithium) are the only elements that occur naturally without the nuclear fusion activity of stars. Thus, the metallicity of a galaxy or other object is an indication of past stellar activity.

Most standard (baryonic) matter is found in the form of atoms or plasma, although there are many other unusual kinds of matter. Other forms of baryonic matter include white dwarfs, neutron stars and black holes. Standard matter also exists as photons (mostly in the cosmic microwave background) and neutrons.

Hydrogen is the most abundant element in the known Universe; helium is second. However, after this, the rank of abundance does not continue to correspond to the atomic number; oxygen has abundance rank 3, but atomic number 8. All others are substantially less common.

The abundance of the lightest elements is well predicted by the standard cosmological model, since they were mostly produced shortly (i.e., within a few hundred seconds) after the Big Bang, in a process known as Big Bang nucleosynthesis. Heavier elements were mostly produced much later, inside stars.

Helium-3 is rare on Earth and sought-after for use in nuclear fusion research. More abundant helium-3 is thought to exist on the Moon. Additional helium is produced by the fusion of hydrogen inside stellar cores by a variety of processes including the proton-proton chain and the CNO cycle.

Ten most common elements in the universe by mass.

Z	Element	Mass fraction in parts per million
1	Hydrogen	7,39,000
2	Helium	2,40,000
8	Oxygen	10,400
6	Carbon	4,600
10	Neon	1,340
26	Iron	1,090
7	Nitrogen	960
14	Silicon	650
12	Magnesium	580
16	Sulfur	440

Elements on Earth

The Earth formed from the same cloud of matter that formed the Sun, but the planets acquired different compositions during the formation and evolution of the solar system. The history of Earth caused parts of this planet to have differing concentrations of the elements.

Abundance of Elements in Earth's Crust

This graph illustrates the relative abundance of the chemical elements in Earth's upper continental crust.

Many of the elements shown in the graphic are classified into (partially overlapping) categories:

- rock-forming elements (major elements in green field and minor elements in light green field);
- rare earth elements (lanthanides, La-Lu, and Y; labeled in blue);
- major industrial metals (global production >~3□107 kg/ year; labeled in bold);

- precious metals (italic);
- the nine rarest "metals" — the six platinum group elements plus Au, Re, and Te (a metalloid).

Note that there are two breaks where the unstable elements technetium (atomic number: 43) and promethium (atomic number: 61) would be. These are very rare, as on Earth they are only produced through the fission of heavy radioactive elements (for example, uranium or thorium). Both elements have been identified spectroscopically in the atmospheres of stars, where they are produced by ongoing nucleosynthetic processes. There are also breaks where the six noble gases would be as they are found in the Earth's crust due to decay chains from radioactive elements and are therefore not included. The six very rare, highly radioactive elements (polonium, astatine, francium, radium, actinium and protactinium) are not included, as their natural abundances are too low to have been accurately measured.

Oxygen and silicon are notably common; they form several common silicate minerals.

"Rare earth" Element Abundances

"Rare" earth elements is a historical misnomer; persistence of the term reflects unfamiliarity rather than true rarity. The more abundant rare earth elements are each similar in crustal concentration to commonplace industrial metals such as chromium, nickel, copper, zinc, molybdenum, tin, tungsten, or lead. Even the two least abundant rare earth elements (Tm, Lu) are nearly 200 times more common than gold. However, in contrast to ordinary base and precious metals, rare earth elements have very little tendency to become concentrated in exploitable ore deposits. Consequently, most of the world's supply of rare earth elements comes from only a handful of sources.

Differences in abundances of individual rare earth elements in the upper continental crust of Earth represent the superposition of two effects, one nuclear and one geochemical. First, rare earth elements with even atomic numbers (58Ce, 60Nd, ...) have greater cosmic and terrestrial abundances than adjacent rare earth elements with odd atomic numbers (57La, 59Pr, ...). Second, the lighter rare earth elements are more incompatible (because they have larger ionic radii) and therefore more strongly concentrated in the continental crust than the heavier rare earth elements. In most rare earth deposits, the first four rare earth elements - La, Ce, Pr, and Nd - constitute 80 to 99% of the total.

Ocean

Elemental Composition of Earth's ocean water (by mass)

Element	Per cent	Element	Per cent
Oxygen	85.84	Sulfur	0.091
Hydrogen	10.82	Calcium	0.04
Chlorine	1.94	Potassium	0.04
Sodium	1.08	Bromine	0.0067
Magnesium	0.1292	Carbon	0.0028

Atmosphere

The order of elements by volume-fraction (which is approximately molecular mole-fraction) in the atmosphere is nitrogen (78.1%), oxygen (20.9%), argon (0.96%), followed by (in uncertain order) carbon and hydrogen because water vapor and carbon dioxide, which represent most of these two elements in the air, are variable components. Sulfur, phosphorus, and all other elements are present in significantly lower proportions.

According to the above argon, a significant if not major component of the atmosphere, does not appear in the crust at all. This is because the atmosphere has a far smaller mass than the crust, so argon remaining in the crust contributes little to mass-fraction there, while at the same time buildup of argon in the atmosphere has become large enough to be significant.

Human Body

By mass, human cells consist of 65-90% water (H_2O) and a significant portion is composed of carbon-containing organic molecules. Oxygen therefore contributes a majority of a human body's mass, followed by carbon. 99% of the mass of the human body is made up of the six elements: oxygen, carbon, hydrogen, nitrogen, calcium and phosphorus.

Element	Per cent by mass
Oxygen	65
Carbon	18
Hydrogen	10
Nitrogen	3
Calcium	1.5
Phosphorus	1.2
Potassium	0.2
Sulfur	0.2
Chlorine	0.2
Sodium	0.1
Magnesium	0.05
Iron, Cobalt, Copper, Zinc, Iodine	<0.05 each
Selenium, Fluorine	<0.01 each

Chemical Treatment of Water

For the chemical treatment of water a great variety of chemicals can be applied. Below, the different types of water treatment chemicals are summed up:

Algaecides

Algaecides are chemicals that kill algae and blue or green algae, when they are added to water. Examples are copper sulphate, iron salts, rosin amine salts and benzalkonium chloride. Algaecides are effective against algae, but are not very usable for algal blooms for environmental reasons. The problem with most algaecides is that they kill all present algae, but they do not remove the toxins that are released by the algae prior to death.

Antifoams

Foam is a mass of bubbles created when certain types of gas are dispersed into a liquid. Strong films of liquid than surround the bubbles, forming large volumes of non-productive foam.

The cause of foam is a complicated study in physical chemistry, but we already know that its existence presents serious problems in both the operation of industrial processes and the quality of finished products. When it is not held under control, foam can reduce the capacity of equipment and increase the duration and costs of processes. Antifoam blends contain oils combined with small amounts of silica. They break down foam thanks to two of silicone's properties: incompatibility with aqueous systems and ease of spreading. Antifoam compounds are available either as powder or as an emulsion of the pure product.

Powder

Antifoam powder covers a group of products based on modified polydimethylsiloxane. The products vary in their basic properties, but as a group they introduce excellent antifoaming in a wide range of applications and conditions. The antifoams are chemically inert and do not react with the medium that is defoamed. They are odourless, tasteless, non-volatile, non-toxic and they do not corrode materials. The only disadvantage of the powdery product is that it cannot be used in watery solutions.

Emulsions

Antifoam Emulsions are aqueous emulsions of polydimethylsiloxane fluids. They have the same properties as the powder form, the only difference is that they can also be applied in watery solutions.

Biocides

In laboratory tests a maximum tolerable microbial population limit in systems in determined. When these data are known in many cases the number of bacteria and other microrganisms needs serious reduction. This can be accomplished by addition to biocides; chemical compounds that are toxic to the present microrganisms. Biocides are usually slug fed to a system to bring about rapid effective population reductions from which the microrganisms cannot easily recover. There are various different biocides, some of which have a wide range of effect on many different kinds of bacteria. They can be divided up into oxidising agents and non-oxidising agents.

Oxidising Agents

- Chlorine
- Chlorine dioxide
- Chloroisocyanurates
- Hypochlorite
- Ozone

Chlorine

Chlorine is the most widely used industrial biocide today. It has been used for disinfection of domestic water supplies and for the removal of tastes and odours from water for a long time. The amount of chlorine that needs to be added in a water system is determined by several factors, namely chlorine demand, contact time, pH and temperature of the water, the volume of water and the amount of chlorine that is most through aeration. When chlorine gas enters a water supply it will hydrolyse to form hypochlorous and hydrochlorous acid. The latter determines the biocidal activity.

This process takes place according to the following reaction:

$$Cl_2 + H_2O \rightarrow HOCl + HCl$$

Hydrochlorous acid is responsible for the oxidation reactions with the cytoplasm of microrganisms, after diffusion through the cell walls. Chlorine than disturbs the production of ATP (adenosine triphosphate), an essential compound for the respiration of microrganisms. The bacteria that are present in the water will die as a consequence of experienced breathing problems, caused by the activity of the chlorine.

The amount of chlorine that needs to be added for the control of bacterial growth is determined by the pH. The higher the pH, the more chlorine is needed to kill the unwanted bacteria in a water system. When the pH values are within a range of 8 to 9, 0.4 ppm of chlorine must be added. When the pH values are within a range of 9 to 10, 0.8 ppm of chlorine must be added.

Chlorine dioxide

Chlorine dioxide is an active oxidising biocide, that is applied more an more due to the fact that is has less damaging effects to the environment and human health than chlorine. It does not form hydrochlorous acids in water; it exists as dissolved chlorine dioxide, a compound that is a more reactive biocide as higher pH ranges.

Chlorine dioxide is an explosive gas, and therefore, it has to be produced or generated on site, by means of the following reactions:

$$Cl_2 + NaClO_2 \rightarrow 2\ NaCl + 2\ ClO_2$$

or

$$2\ HCl + 3\ NaOCl + NaClO_2 \rightarrow 2\ ClO_2 + 4\ NaCl + H_2O$$

Chloroisocyanurates

These are organo-chlorine compounds that will hydrolyse into hypochlorous acid and cyanuric acid in water. The cyanuric acid reduces chlorine loss due to photochemical reactions with UV-light, so that more hydrochlorous acid will originate and the biocidal action will be enhanced.

Hypochlorite

Hypochlorite is salt from hypochlorous acid. It is formulated in several different forms. Usually hypochlorite is applied as sodium hypochlorite (NaOCl) and calcium hypochlorite (Ca(OCl)2). These compounds can be applied as biocides. They function in very much the same way as chlorine, although they are a bit less effective.

Ozone

Ozone is naturally instable. It can be used as a powerful oxidising agent, when it is generated in a reactor. As a biocide it acts in much the same way as chlorine; it disturbs the formation of ATP, so that the cell respiration of microorganisms will be made difficult. During oxidation with ozone, bacteria usually die from loss of life-sustaining cytoplasm.

While the oxidation process takes place ozone parts into *oxygen* and an *ozone* atom, which is lost during the reaction with cell fluids of the bacteria:

$$O_3 \rightarrow O_2 + (O)$$

A number of factors determine the amount of ozone required during oxidation, these are pH, temperature, organics and solvents and accumulated reaction products.

Ozone is more environmentally friendly than chlorine, because it does not add chlorine to the water system. Due to its decomposition to oxygen it will not harm aquatic life.

Usually 0.5 ppm of ozone is added to a water system, either on continuous or intermittent basis.

Non-oxidising Agents

- Acrolein
- Amines
- Chlorinated phenolics
- Copper salts
- Organo-sulphur compounds
- Quaternary ammonium salts

In many cases oxidising agents are not effective biocides. Non-oxidising agents are than applied.

Acrolein

Acrolein is an extremely effective biocide that has an environmental advantage over oxidising biocides, because it can easily be deactivated by sodium sulphite before discharge to a receiving stream.

Acrolein has the ability to attack and distort protein groups and enzyme synthesis reactions. It is usually fed to water systems as a gas in amounts of 0.1 to 0.2 ppm in neutral to slightly alkaline water.

Acrolein is not used very frequently, as it is extremely flammable and also toxic.

Amines

Amines are effective surfactants that can act as biocides due to their ability to kill microrganisms. They can enhance the biocidal effect to chlorinate phenolics when they are applied in water.

Chlorinated Phenolics

Chlorinated phenolics, unlike oxidising biocides, have no effect on respiration of microrganisms. However, they do induce growth. The chlorinated phenolics first adsorb to the cell wall of microrganisms by interaction with hydrogen bonds. After adsorption to the cell wall they will diffuse into the cell where they go into suspension and precipitate proteins. Due to this mechanism the growth of the microorganisms is inhibited.

Copper Salts

Copper salts have been used as biocides for a long time, but their use has been limited in recent years due to concerns about heavy metal contamination. They are applied in amounts of 1 to 2 ppm.

When the water is treated is located in steel tanks copper salts should not be applied, because of their ability to corrode steel. Copper salts should not be used in water that will be applied as drinking water either, because they are toxic to humans.

Organo-sulphur Compounds

Organo-sulphur compounds act as biocides by inhibiting cell growth. There are a variety of different organo-suplhur compounds that function in different pH ranges.

Normally energy is transferred in bacterial cells when iron reacts from Fe^{3+} to Fe^{2+}. Organo-sulphur compounds remove the Fe^{3+} by complexion as an iron salt. The transfer of energy through the cells is than stopped and immediate cell death will follow.

Quaternary Ammonium Salts

Quaternary ammonium salts are surface-active chemicals that consist generally of one nitrogen atom, surrounded by substitutes containing eight to twenty-five carbon atoms on four sights of the nitrogen atom.

These compounds are generally most effective against bacteria in alkaline pH ranges. They are positively charged and will bond to the negatively charged sites on the bacterial cell wall. These electrostatic bonds will cause the bacteria to die of stress in the cell wall. They also cause the normal flow of life-sustaining compounds through the cell wall to stop, by declining its permeability.

Use of quaternary ammonium salts is limited, due to their interaction with oil when this is present and the fact that they can cause foaming.

Boiler Water Chemicals

Boiler water chemicals include all chemicals that are used for the following applications:

- Oxygen scavenging;
- Scale inhibition;
- Corrosion inhibition;
- Antifoaming;
- Alkalinity control.

Coagulants

When referring to coagulants, positive ions with high valence are preferred. Generally aluminium and iron are applied, aluminium as $Al_2(SO_4)^{3-}$ (aluin) and iron as either $FeCl_3$ or $Fe_2(SO_4)^{3-}$. One can also apply the relatively cheap form $FeSO_4$, on condition that it will be oxidised to Fe^{3+} during aeration.

Coagulation is very dependent on the doses of coagulants, the pH and colloid concentrations. To adjust pH levels $Ca(OH)_2$ is applied as co-flocculent. Doses usually vary between 10 and 90 mg Fe^{3+} / L, but when salts are present a higher dose needs to be applied.

Corrosion Inhibitors

Corrosion is a general term that indicates the conversion of a metal into a soluble compound. Corrosion can lead to failure of critical parts of boiler systems, deposition of corrosion products in critical heat exchange areas, and overall efficiency loss. That is why corrosion inhibitors are often applied. Inhibitors are chemicals that react with a metallic surface, giving the surface a certain level of protection. Inhibitors often work by adsorbing themselves on the metallic surface, protecting the metallic surface by forming a film. There are five different kinds of corrosion inhibitors. These are:

1. Passivity inhibitors (passivators). These cause a shift of the corrosion potential, forcing the metallic surface into the passive range. Examples of passivity inhibitors are oxidizing anions, such as chromate, nitrite and nitrate

and non-oxidizing ions such as phosphate and molybdate. These inhibitors are the most effective and consequently the most widely used.

2. Cathodic inhibitors. Some cathodic inhibitors, such as compounds of arsenic and antimony, work by making the recombination and discharge of hydrogen more difficult. Other cathodic inhibitors, ions such as calcium, zinc or magnesium, may be precipitated as oxides to form a protective layer on the metal.

3. Organic inhibitors. These affect the entire surface of a corroding metal when present in certain concentration. Organic inhibitors protect the metal by forming a hydrophobic film on the metal surface. Organic inhibitors will be adsorbed according to the ionic charge of the inhibitor and the charge on the surface.

4. Precipitation inducing inhibitors. These are compounds that cause the formation of precipitates on the surface of the metal, thereby providing a protective film.

   The most common inhibitors of this category are silicates and phosphates.

5. Volatile Corrosion Inhibitors (VCI). These are compounds transported in a closed environment to the site of corrosion by volatilisation from a source. Examples are morpholine and hydrazine and volatile solids such as salts of dicyclohexylamine, cyclohexylamine and hexamethylene-amine. On contact with the metal surface, the vapour of these salts condenses and is hydrolysed by moist, to liberate protective ions.

Disinfectants

Disinfectants kill present unwanted microrganisms in water. There are various different types of disinfectants:

- Chlorine (dose 2-10 mg/L)
- Chlorine dioxide

- Hypochlorite
- Ozone

Chlorine dioxide Disinfection

ClO_2 is used principally as a primary disinfectant for surface waters with odor and taste problems. It is an effective biocide at concentrations as low as 0.1 ppm and over a wide pH range. ClO_2 penetrates the bacterial cell wall and reacts with vital amino acids in the cytoplasm of the cell to kill the organisms. The by-product of this reaction is chlorite.

Chlorine dioxide disinfects according to the same principle as chlorine, however, as opposed to chlorine, chlorine dioxide has no harmful effects on human health.

Hypochlorite Disinfection

Hypochlorite is aplied in the same way as chlorine dioxide and chlorine. Hypo chlorination is a disinfection method that is not used widely anymore, since an environmental agency proved that the Hypochlorite for disinfection in water was the cause of bromate consistence in water.

Ozone Disinfection

Ozone is a very strong oxidation medium, with a remarkably short life span. It consists of oxygen molecules with an extra O-atom, to form O_3. When ozone comes in contact with odour, bacteria or viruses the extra O-atom breaks them down directly, by means of oxidation. The third O-atom of the ozone molecules is than lost and only oxygen will remain.

Disinfectants can be used in various industries. Ozone is used in the pharmaceutical industry, for drinking water preparation, for treatment of process water, for preparation of ultra-pure water and for surface disinfection.

Chlorine dioxide is used primarily for drinking water preparation and disinfection of piping.

Flocculants

To promote the formation of flocs in water that contains suspended solids polymer flocculants (polyelectrolytes) are applied to promote bonds formation between particles. These polymers have a very specific effect, dependent upon their charges, their molar weight and their molecular degree of ramification. The polymers are water-soluble and their molar weight varies between 105 and 106 g/ mol.

There can be several charges on one flocculent. There are cationic polymers, based on nitrogen, anionic polymers, based on carboxylate ions and polyampholytes, which carry both positive and negative charges.

Neutralizing Agents (Alkalinity Control)

In order to neutralize acids and basics we use either sodium hydroxide solution (NaOH), calcium carbonate, or lime suspension ($Ca(OH)_2$) to increase pH levels. We use diluted sulphuric acid (H_2SO_4) or diluted hydrochloric acid (HCl) to decline pH levels. The dose of neutralizing agents depends upon the pH of the water in a reaction basin. Neutralization reactions cause a rise in temperature.

Oxidants

Chemical oxidation processes use (chemical) oxidants to reduce COD/BOD levels, and to remove both organic and oxidisable inorganic components. The processes can completely oxidise organic materials to carbon dioxide and water, although it is often not necessary to operate the processes to this level of treatment. A wide variety of oxidation chemicals are available. Examples are:

- Hydrogen peroxide;
- Ozone;
- Combined ozone & peroxide;
- Oxygen.

Hydrogen Peroxide

Hydrogen peroxide is widely used thanks to its properties; it is a safe, effective, powerful and versatile oxidant. The main applications of H_2O_2 are oxidation to aid odour control and corrosion control, organic oxidation, metal oxidation and toxicity oxidation. The most difficult pollutants to oxidize may require H_2O_2 to be activated with catalysts such as iron, copper, manganese or other transition metal compounds.

Ozone

Ozone cannot only be applied as a disinfectant; it can also aid the removal of contaminants from water by means of oxidation. Ozone then purifies water by breaking up organic contaminants and converting inorganic contaminants to an insoluble form that can then be filtered out. The Ozone system can remove up to twenty-five contaminants. Chemicals that can be oxidized with ozone are:

- Absorbable organic halogens;
- Nitrite;
- Iron;
- Manganese;
- Cyanide;
- Pesticides;
- Nitrogen oxides;
- Odorous substances;
- Chlorinated hydrocarbons;
- PCB's.

Oxygen

Oxygen can also be applied as an oxidant, for instance to realize the oxidation of iron and manganese. The reactions that occur during oxidation by oxygen are usually quite similar.

These are the reactions of the oxidation of iron and manganese with oxygen:

$$2\ Fe^{2+} + O_2 + 2\ OH^- \rightarrow Fe_2O_3 + H_2O$$

$$2\ Mn^{2+} + O_2 + 4\ OH^- \rightarrow 2\ MnO_2 + 2\ H_2O$$

Oxygen Scavengers

Oxygen scavenging means preventing oxygen from introducing oxidation reactions. Most of the naturally occurring organics have a slightly negative charge. Due to that they can absorb oxygen molecules, because these carry a slightly positive charge, to prevent oxidation reactions from taking place in water and other liquids.

Oxygen scavengers include both volatile products, such as hydrazine (N_2H_4) or other organic products like carbohydrazine, hydroquinone, diethylhydroxyethanol, methylethylketoxime, but also non-volatile salts, such as sodium sulphite (Na_2SO_3) and other inorganic compounds, or derivatives thereof. The salts often contain catalysing compounds to increase the rate of reaction with dissolved oxygen, for instance cobalt chloride.

pH Conditioners

Municipal water is often pH-adjusted, in order to prevent corrosion from pipes and to prevent dissolution of lead into water supplies. During water treatment pH adjustments may also be required. The pH is brought up or down through addition of basics or acids. An example of lowering the pH is the addition of hydrogen chloride, in case of a basic liquid. An example of bringing up the pH is the addition of natrium hydroxide, in case of an acidic liquid.

The pH will be converted to approximately seven to seven and a half, after addition of certain concentrations of acids or basics. The concentration of the substance and the kind of substance that is added, depend upon the necessary decrease or increase of the pH.

Resin Cleaners

Ion exchange resins need to be regenerated after application, after that, they can be reused. But every time the ion exchangers are used serious fouling takes place. The contaminants that enter the resins will not be removed through regeneration; therefore resins need cleaning with certain chemicals. Chemicals that are used are for instance sodium chloride, potassium chloride, citric acid and chlorine dioxide. Chlorine dioxide cleansing serves the removal of organic contaminants on ion exchange resins. Prior to every cleaning treatment resins should be regenerated. After that, in case chlorine dioxide is used, 500 ppm of chlorine dioxide in solution is passed through the resin bed and oxidises the contaminants.

Scale Inhibitors

Scale is the precipitate that forms on surfaces in contact with water as a result of the precipitation of normally soluble solids that become insoluble as temperature increases. Some examples of scale are calcium carbonate, calcium sulphate, and calcium silicate.

Scale inhibitors are surface-active negatively charged polymers. As minerals exceed their solubility's and begin to merge, the polymers become attached. The structure for crystallisation is disrupted and the formation of scale is prevented. The particles of scale combined with the inhibitor will than be dispersed and remain in suspension.

Examples of scale inhibitors are phosphate esters, phosphoric acid and solutions of low molecular weight polyacrylic acid.

WATER POLLUTION

Water pollution is the contamination of water bodies such as lakes, rivers, oceans, and groundwater caused by human activities, which can be harmful to organisms and plants that live in these water bodies.

Introduction

Water pollution is a major problem in the global context. It has been suggested that it is the leading worldwide cause of deaths and diseases, and that it accounts for the deaths of more than 14,000 people daily. In addition to the acute problems of water pollution in developing countries, industrialized countries continue to struggle with pollution problems as well. In the most recent national report on water quality in the United States, 45 percent of assessed stream miles, 47 percent of assessed lake acres, and 32 percent of assessed bay and estuarine square miles were classified as polluted.

Water is typically referred to as polluted when it is impaired by anthropogenic contaminants and either does not support a human use, like serving as drinking water, and/or undergoes a marked shift in its ability to support its constituent biotic communities, such as fish. Natural phenomena such as volcanoes, algae blooms, storms, and earthquakes also cause major changes in water quality and the ecological status of water. Water pollution has many causes and characteristics.

Water Pollution Categories

Surface water and groundwater have often been studied and managed as separate resources, although they are interrelated. Sources of surface water pollution are generally grouped into two categories based on their origin.

Point Source Pollution

Point source pollution refers to contaminants that enter a waterway through a discrete conveyance, such as a pipe or ditch. Examples of sources in this category include discharges from a sewage treatment plant, a factory, or a city storm drain. The U.S. Clean Water Act (CWA) defines point source for regulatory enforcement purposes.

Non-point Source Pollution

Non-point source (NPS) pollution refers to diffuse contamination that does not originate from a single discrete source. NPS pollution is often a cumulative effect of small amounts of contaminants gathered from a large area. Nutrient runoff in stormwater from "sheet flow" over an agricultural field or a forest are sometimes cited as examples of NPS pollution.

Contaminated stormwater washed off of parking lots, roads and highways, called urban runoff, is sometimes included under the category of NPS pollution. However, this runoff is typically channeled into storm drain systems and discharged through pipes to local surface waters, and is a point source. The CWA definition of point source was amended in 1987 to include municipal storm sewer systems, as well as industrial stormwater, such as from construction sites

Groundwater Pollution

Interactions between groundwater and surface water are complex. Consequently, groundwater pollution, sometimes referred to as *groundwater contamination*, is not as easily classified as surface water pollution. By its very nature, groundwater aquifers are susceptible to contamination from sources that may not directly affect surface water bodies, and the distinction of point vs. nonpoint source may be irrelevant. A spill of a chemical contaminant on soil, located away from a surface water body, may not necessarily create point source or non-point source pollution, but nonetheless may contaminate the aquifer below. Analysis of groundwater contamination may focus on soil characteristics and hydrology, as well as the nature of the contaminant itself.

Causes of Water Pollution

The specific contaminants leading to pollution in water include a wide spectrum of chemicals, pathogens, and physical or sensory changes such as elevated temperature and discoloration. While many of the chemicals and substances that are regulated may be naturally occurring (calcium, sodium, iron, manganese, etc.) the concentration is often the key in determining what is a natural component of water, and what is a contaminant.

Oxygen-depleting substances may be natural materials, such as plant matter (e.g. leaves and grass) as well as man-made chemicals. Other natural and anthropogenic substances may cause turbidity (cloudiness) which blocks light and disrupts plant growth, and clogs the gills of some fish species.

Many of the chemical substances are toxic. Pathogens can produce waterborne diseases in either human or animal hosts. Alteration of water's physical chemistry include acidity (change in pH), electrical conductivity, temperature, and eutrophication. Eutrophication is the fertilization of surface water by nutrients that were previously scarce.

Pathogens

Coliform bacteria are a commonly-used bacterial indicator of water pollution, although not an actual cause of disease. Other microorganisms sometimes found in surface waters which have caused human health problems include:

- Cryptosporidium parvum
- Giardia lamblia
- Salmonella
- Novovirus and other viruses
- Parasitic worms (helminths)

High levels of pathogens may result from inadequately treated sewage discharges This can be caused by a sewage plant designed with less than secondary treatment (more typical in less-developed countries). In developed countries, older cities with aging infrastructure may have leaky sewage collection systems (pipes, pumps, valves), which can cause sanitary sewer overflows. Some cities also have combined sewers, which may discharge untreated sewage during rain storms.

Pathogen discharges may also be caused by poorly-managed livestock operations.

Chemical and Other Contaminants

Muddy river polluted by sediment. Photo courtesy of United States Geological Survey. Contaminants may include organic and inorganic substances.

Organic water pollutants include:

Detergents

- *Disinfection by-products* found in chemically disinfected drinking water, such as chloroform
- *Food processing* waste, which can include oxygen-demanding substances, fats and grease.
- *Insecticides* and *herbicides*, a huge range of organohalides and other chemical compounds.
- *Petroleum hydrocarbons*, including fuels (gasoline, diesel fuel, jet fuels, and fuel oil) and lubricants (motor oil), and fuel combustion byproducts, from stormwater runoff.
- *Tree* and brush debris from *logging* operations.
- *Volatile organic compounds* (VOCs), such as industrial solvents, from improper storage. Chlorinated solvents, which are dense non-aqueous phase liquids (DNAPLs), may fall to the bottom of reservoirs, since they don't mix well with water and are denser.
- Various chemical compounds found in personal *hygiene* and *cosmetic* products.

Inorganic water pollutants include:

- *Acidity* caused by industrial discharges (especially sulfur dioxide from power plants).
- *Ammonia* from food processing waste.

- *Chemical waste* as industrial by-products.
- *Fertilizers* containing nutrients—nitrates and phosphates—which are found in stormwater runoff from agriculture, as well as commercial and residential use.
- *Heavy metals* from *motor vehicles* (via urban stormwater runoff) and acid mine drainage.
- *Silt* (*sediment*) in runoff from construction sites, logging, slash and burn practices or land clearing sites.

Macroscopic pollution—large visible items polluting the water—may be termed "floatables" in an urban stormwater context, or marine debris when found on the open seas, and can include such items as:

- *Trash* (e.g. paper, plastic, or food waste) discarded by people on the ground, and that are washed by rainfall into storm drains and eventually discharged into surface waters.
- *Nurdles,* small ubiquitous waterborne plastic pellets.
- *Shipwrecks,* large derelict ships.

Transport and Chemical Reactions of Water Pollutants

Most water pollutants are eventually carried by rivers into the oceans. In some areas of the world the influence can be traced hundred miles from the mouth by studies using hydrology transport models. Advanced computer models such as SWMM or the DSSAM Model have been used in many locations worldwide to examine the fate of pollutants in aquatic systems. Indicator filter feeding species such as copepods have also been used to study pollutant fates in the New York Bight, for example. The highest toxin loads are not directly at the mouth of the Hudson River, but 100 kilometers south, since several days are required for incorporation into planktonic tissue. The Hudson discharge flows south along the coast due to coriolis force. Further south then are areas of oxygen depletion, caused by chemicals using up oxygen and by algae blooms, caused by excess nutrients from algal cell death and decomposition. Fish and shellfish kills have been reported, because toxins climb the food chain after small fish consume copepods, then large fish eat smaller fish, etc. Each successive step up the food chain causes a stepwise concentration of pollutants such as heavy metals (e.g. mercury) and persistent organic pollutants such as DDT. This is known as biomagnification, which is occasionally used interchangeably with bioaccumulation.

Large gyres (vortexes) in the oceans trap floating plastic debris. The North Pacific Gyre for example has collected the so-called "Great Pacific Garbage Patch" that is now estimated at 100 times the size of Texas. Many of these long-lasting pieces wind up in the stomachs of marine birds and animals. This results in obstruction of digestive pathways which leads to reduced appetite or even starvation.

Many chemicals undergo reactive decay or chemically change especially over long periods of time in groundwater reservoirs. A noteworthy class of such chemicals is the chlorinated hydrocarbons such as trichloroethylene (used in industrial metal degreasing and electronics manufacturing) and tetrachloroethylene used in the dry cleaning industry (note latest advances in liquid carbon dioxide in dry cleaning that avoids all use of chemicals). Both of these chemicals, which are carcinogens themselves, undergo partial decomposition reactions, leading to new hazardous chemicals (including dichloroethylene and vinyl chloride).

Groundwater pollution is much more difficult to abate than surface pollution because groundwater can move great distances through unseen aquifers. Non-porous aquifers such as clays partially purify water of bacteria by simple filtration (adsorption and absorption), dilution, and, in some cases, chemical reactions and biological activity: however, in some cases, the pollutants merely transform to soil contaminants. Groundwater that moves through cracks and caverns is not filtered and can be transported as easily as surface water. In fact, this can be aggravated by the human tendency to use natural sinkholes as dumps in areas of Karst topography.

There are a variety of secondary effects stemming not from the original pollutant, but a derivative condition. Some of these secondary impacts are:

- Silt-bearing surface runoff from can inhibit the penetration of sunlight through the water column, hampering photosynthesis in aquatic plants.
- Thermal pollution can induce fish kills and invasion by new thermophilic species. This can cause further problems to existing wildlife.

Measurement of Water Pollution

Water pollution may be analyzed through several broad categories of methods: physical, chemical and biological. Most methods involve collection of samples, followed by specialized analytical tests. Some methods may be conducted in situ, without sampling, such as temperature. Government agencies and research organizations have published standardized, validated analytical test methods to facilitate the comparability of results from disparate testing events.

Sampling

Sampling of water for physical or chemical testing can be done by several methods, depending on the accuracy needed and the characteristics of the contaminant. Many contamination events are sharply restricted in time, most commonly in association with rain events. For this reason "grab" samples are often inadequate for fully quantifying contaminant levels. Scientists gathering this type of data often employ auto-sampler devices that pump increments of water at either time or discharge intervals.

Sampling for biological testing involves collection of plants and/or animals from the surface water body.

Depending on the type of assessment, the organisms may be identified for biosurveys (population counts) and returned to the water body, or they may be dissected for bioassays to determine toxicity.

Physical Testing

Common physical tests of water include temperature, solids concentration and turbidity.

Chemical Testing

Water samples may be examined using the principles of analytical chemistry. Many published test methods are available for both organic and inorganic compounds. Frequently-used methods include pH, biochemical oxygen demand (BOD), chemical oxygen demand (COD), nutrients (nitrate and phosphorus compounds), metals (including copper, zinc, cadmium, lead and mercury), oil and grease, total petroleum hydrocarbons (TPH), and pesticides.

Biological Testing

Biological testing involves the use of plant, animal, and/or microbial indicators to monitor the health of an aquatic ecosystem.

Control of Water Pollution

Domestic Sewage

In urban areas, domestic sewage is typically treated by centralized sewage treatment plants. In the U.S., most of these plants are operated by local government agencies. Municipal treatment plants are designed to control conventional pollutants: BOD and suspended solids. Well-designed and operated systems (i.e., secondary treatment or better) can remove 90 percent or more of these pollutants. Some plants have additional sub-systems to treat nutrients and pathogens. Most municipal plants are not designed to treat toxic pollutants found in industrial wastewater.

Cities with sanitary sewer overflows or combined sewer overflows employ one or more engineering approaches to reduce discharges of untreated sewage, including:

- utilizing a *green infrastructure* approach to improve stormwater management capacity throughout the system;
- repair and replacement of leaking and malfunctioning equipment;
- increasing overall hydraulic capacity of the sewage collection system (often a very expensive option).

A household or business not served by a municipal treatment plant may have an individual septic tank, which treats the wastewater on site and discharges into the soil. Alternatively, domestic wastewater may be sent to a nearby privately-owned treatment system (e.g. in a rural community).

Industrial Wastewater

Some industrial facilities generate ordinary domestic sewage that can be treated by municipal facilities. Industries that generate wastewater with high concentrations of conventional pollutants (e.g oil and grease), toxic pollutants (e.g. heavy metals, volatile organic compounds) or other nonconventional pollutants such as ammonia, need specialized treatment systems. Some of these facilities can install a pre-treatment system to remove the toxic components, and then send the partially-treated wastewater to the municipal system. Industries generating large volumes of wastewater typically operate their own complete on-site treatment systems.

Some industries have been successful at redesigning their manufacturing processes to reduce or eliminate pollutants, through a process called pollution prevention.

Agricultural Wastewater

Specialized treatment systems are used to treat animal waste and silage by-products.

Construction Site Stormwater

Sediment (loose soil) from construction sites is managed by installation of:

- erosion controls, such as mulching; and
- sediment controls, such as sediment basins and silt fences.

Discharge of toxic chemicals such as motor fuels and concrete washout is prevented by use of:

- spill prevention and control plans; and
- specially-designed containers (e.g. for concrete washout) and structures such as overflow controls and diversion berms.

Urban Runoff (Stormwater)

Effective control of urban runoff involves reducing the velocity and flow of stormwater, as well as reducing pollutant discharges. Local governments use a variety of stormwater management techniques to reduce the effects of urban runoff. These techniques, called best management practices (BMPs) in the U.S., may focus on water quantity control, while others focus on improving water quality, and some perform both functions.

Regulatory Framework

In developed countries, the primary focus of legislation and efforts to curb water pollution for the past several decades was first aimed at point sources. As many point sources have been effectively regulated—principally factories and sewage treatment plants—greater attention has been placed on controlling municipal and industrial stormwater discharges, and NPS contributions.

United Kingdom

In the UK there are common law rights (civil rights) to protect the passage of water across land unfettered in either quality of quantity. Criminal laws dating back to the 16th century exercised some control over water pollution but it was not until the Rivers (Prevention of pollution) Acts 1951-1961 were enacted that any systematic control over water pollution was established. These laws were strengthened and extended in the Control of Pollution Act 1984 which has since been updated and modified by a series of further acts. It is a criminal offence to either pollute a lake, river, groundwater or the sea or to discharge any liquid into such water bodies without proper authority. In England and Wales such permission can only be issued by the Environment Agency and in Scotland by SEPA.

United States

In the USA, concern over water pollution resulted in the enactment of state anti-pollution laws in the latter half of the 19th century, and federal legislation enacted in 1899. The Refuse Act of the federal Rivers and Harbors Act of 1899 prohibits the disposal of any refuse matter from into either the nation's navigable rivers, lakes, streams, and other navigable bodies of water, or any tributary to such waters, unless one has first obtained a permit. The Water Pollution Control Act, passed in 1948, gave authority to the Surgeon General to reduce water pollution. However, this law did not lead to major reductions in pollution.

Growing public awareness and concern for controlling water pollution led Congress to carry out a major re-write of water pollution law in 1972. The Federal Water Pollution Control Act Amendments of 1972, commonly known as the Clean Water Act (CWA), established the basic mechanisms for controlling point source pollution. The law mandated the United States Environmental Protection Agency (EPA) to publish and enforce wastewater standards for industry and municipal sewage treatment plants. The Act also continued requirements that EPA and states issue water quality standards for surface water bodies. Congress included authorization in the Act for major public financing to build municipal sewage treatment plants. The 1972 CWA, however, did not require similar regulatory standards for non-point sources.

In 1987, Congress expanded the coverage of the CWA with enactment of the Water Quality Act These amendments defined both municipal and industrial stormwater discharges as point sources and required these facilities to obtain discharge permits. The 1987 law also re-organized the public financing of municipal treatment projects and created a non-point source demonstration grant program. Further amplification of the CWA included the enactment of the Great Lakes Legacy Act of 2002.

10

Natural Environment

The natural environment, commonly referred to simply as the environment, is a term that encompasses all living and non-living things occurring naturally on Earth or some region thereof.

Terminology and Concept

The concept of the natural environment can be broken down into a few key components.

Complete ecological units that function as natural systems without massive human intervention, including all vegetation, animals, microorganisms, soil, rocks, atmosphere and natural phenomena that occur within their boundaries.

Universal natural resources and physical phenomena that lack clear-cut boundaries, such as air, water, and climate, as well as energy, radiation, electric charge, and magnetism, not originating from human activity.

The natural environment is contrasted with the built environment, which comprises the areas and components that are strongly influenced by humans. A geographical area is regarded as a natural environment (with an indefinite article), if the human impact on it is kept under a certain limited level (similar to section 1 above). This level depends on the specific context, and changes in different areas and contexts. The term wilderness, on the other hand, refers to Earth that has not been modified by human activity.

Composition

Earth science (also known as geoscience, the geosciences or the Earth Sciences), is an all-embracing term for the sciences related to the planet Earth There are four major disciplines in earth sciences, namely geography, geology, geophysics and geodesy. These major disciplines use physics, chemistry, biology, chronology and mathematics to build a qualitative and quantitative understanding of the principal areas or spheres of the Earth system. Earth science generally recognizes 4 spheres, the lithosphere, the hydrosphere, the atmosphere, and the biosphere ; these correspond to rocks, water, air, and life. Some practitioners include, as part of the spheres of the Earth, the cryosphere (corresponding to ice) as a distinct portion of the hydrosphere, as well as the pedosphere (corresponding to soil) as an active and intermixed sphere.

Geological Activity

The Earth's crust, or Continental crust, is the outermost solid land surface of the planet, is chemically and mechanically different from underlying mantles, and has been generated largely by igneous processes in which magma (molten rock) cools and solidifies to form solid land. Plate tectonics, mountain ranges, volcanoes, and earthquakes are geological phenomena that can be explained in terms of energy transformations in the Earth's crust and might be thought of as the process by which the earth resurfaces itself. Beneath the Earth's crust lies the mantle which is heated by the radioactive decay of heavy elements. The mantle is not quite solid and consists of magma which is in a state of semi-perpetual convection. This convection process causes the lithospheric plates to move, albeit slowly. The resulting process is known as plate tectonics. Volcanoes result primarily from the melting of subducted crust material. Crust material that is forced into the Asthenosphere melts, and some portion of the melted material becomes light enough to rise to the surface, giving birth to volcanoes.

Oceanic Activity

An ocean is a major body of saline water, and a principal component of the hydrosphere. Approximately 71% of the Earth's surface (an area of some 361 million square kilometers) is covered by ocean, a continuous body of water that is customarily divided into several principal oceans and smaller seas. More than half of this area is over 3,000 meters (9,800 ft) deep. Average oceanic salinity is around 35 parts per thousand (ppt) (3.5%), and nearly all seawater has a salinity in the range of 30 to 38 ppt. Though generally recognized as several 'separate' oceans, these waters comprise one global, interconnected body of salt water often referred to as the World Ocean or global ocean. This concept of a global ocean as a continuous body of water with relatively free interchange among its parts is of fundamental importance to oceanography.

The major oceanic divisions are defined in part by the continents, various archipelagos, and other criteria: these divisions are (in descending order of size) the Pacific Ocean, the Atlantic Ocean, the Indian Ocean, the Southern Ocean (which is sometimes subsumed as the southern portions of the Pacific, Atlantic, and Indian Oceans), and the Arctic Ocean (which is sometimes considered a sea of the Atlantic). The Pacific and Atlantic may be further subdivided by the equator into northerly and southerly portions. Smaller regions of the oceans are called seas, gulfs, bays and other names. There are also salt lakes, which are smaller bodies of landlocked saltwater that are not interconnected with the World Ocean. Two notable examples of salt lakes are the Aral Sea and the Great Salt Lake.

Atmosphere, Climate and Weather

The atmosphere of the Earth serves as a key factor in sustaining the planetary ecosystem. The thin layer of gases that envelops the Earth is held in place by the planet's gravity. Dry air consists of 78% nitrogen, 21% oxygen, 1% argon and other inert gases, carbon dioxide, etc.; but air also contains a variable amount of water vapor. The atmospheric pressure declines steadily with altitude, and has a scale height of about 8 kilometres at the Earth's surface: the height at which the atmospheric pressure has declined by a factor of e (a mathematical constant equal to 2.71...) The ozone layer of the Earth's atmosphere plays an important role in depleting the amount of ultraviolet (UV) radiation that reaches the surface. As DNA is readily damaged by UV light, this serves to protect life at the surface. The atmosphere also retains heat during the night, thereby reducing the daily temperature extremes.

Effect of Global Warming

The potential dangers of global warming are being increasingly studied by a wide global consortium of scientists, who are increasingly concerned about the potential long-term effects of global warming on our natural environment and on the planet. Of particular concern is how climate change and global warming caused by anthropogenic, or human-made releases of greenhouse gases, most notably carbon dioxide, can act interactively, and have adverse effects upon the planet, it's natural environment and humans' existence. Efforts have been increasingly focused on the mitigation of greenhouse gases that are causing climatic changes, on developing adaptative strategies to global warming, to assist humans, animal and plant species, ecosystems, regions and nations in adjusting to the effects of global warming. Some examples of recent collaboration to address climate change and global warming include:

- The United Nations Framework Convention Treaty and convention on Climate Change, to stabilize greenhouse gas concentrations in the atmosphere at a level that would prevent dangerous anthropogenic interference with the climate system.
- The Kyoto Protocol, which is the protocol to the international Framework Convention on Climate Change treaty, again with the objective of reducing greenhouse gases in an effort to prevent anthropogenic climate change.
- The Western Climate Initiative, to identify, evaluate, and implement collective and cooperative ways to reduce greenhouse gases in the region, focusing on a market-based cap-and-trade system.

A significantly profound challenge is to identify the natural environmental dynamics in contrast to environmental changes not within natural variances. A common solution is to adapt a static view neglecting natural variances to exist. Methodologically, this view could be defended when looking at processes which change slowly and short time series, while the problem arrives when fast processes turns essential in the object of the study.

Life

Although there is no universal agreement on the definition of life, scientists generally accept that the biological manifestation of life is characterized by organization, metabolism, growth, adaptation, response to stimuli and reproduction Life may also be said to be simply the characteristic state of organisms.

Properties common to terrestrial organisms (plants, animals, fungi, protists, archaea and bacteria) are that they are cellular, carbon-and-water-based with complex organization, having a metabolism, a capacity to grow, respond to stimuli, and reproduce. An entity with these properties is generally considered life. However, not every definition of life considers all of these properties to be essential. Human-made analogs of life may also be considered to be life.

Phere is the part of Earth's outer shell — including air, land, surface rocks and water — within which life occurs, and which biotic processes in turn alter or transform. From the broadest geophysiological point of view, the biosphere is the global ecological system integrating all living beings and their relationships, including their interaction with the elements of the lithosphere (rocks), hydrosphere (water), and atmosphere (air). Currently the entire Earth contains over 75 billion tons (150 trillion pounds or about 6.8 x 1013 kilograms) of biomass (life), which lives within various environments within the biosphere.

Ecosystems

A coral reef near the Hawaiian islands is an example of a complex marine ecosystem.An ecosystem is a natural unit consisting of all plants, animals and micro-organisms (biotic factors) in an area functioning together with all of the non-living physical (abiotic) factors of the environment.

Central to the ecosystem concept is the idea that living organisms are continually engaged in a highly interrelated set of relationships with every other element constituting the environment in which they exist. Eugene Odum, one of the founders of the science of ecology, stated: "Any unit that includes all of the organisms (ie: the "community") in a given area interacting with the physical environment so that a flow of energy leads to clearly defined trophic structure, biotic diversity, and material cycles (ie: exchange of materials between living and nonliving parts) within the system is an ecosystem." The human ecosystem concept is then grounded in the deconstruction of the human/nature dichotomy, and the emergent premise that all species are ecologically integrated with each other, as well as with the abiotic constituents of their biotope.

Ecosystems can be bounded and discussed with tremendous variety of scope, and describe any situation where there is relationship between organisms and their environment. If humans are part of the organisms, one can speak of a 'human ecosystem'. As virtually no surface of the earth today is free of human contact, all ecosystems can be more accurately considered as human ecosystems, or more neutrally as human-influenced ecoystems.

Biomes

Biomes are terminologically similar to the concept of ecosystems, and are climatically and geographically defined areas of ecologically similar climatic conditions such as communities of plants, animals, and soil organisms, often referred to as ecosystems. Biomes are defined based on factors such as plant structures (such as trees, shrubs, and grasses), leaf types (such as broadleaf and needleleaf), plant spacing (forest, woodland, savanna), and climate. Unlike ecozones, biomes are not defined by genetic, taxonomic, or historical similarities. Biomes are often identified with particular patterns of ecological succession and climax vegetation.

The High Peaks Wilderness Area in the 6,000,000-acre (2,400,000 ha) Adirondack Park.

Wilderness

Wilderness is generally defined as a natural environment on Earth that has not been significantly modified by human activity. The WILD Foundation goes into more detail, defining wilderness as: "The most intact, undisturbed wild natural areas left on our planet - those last truly wild places that humans do not control and have not developed with roads, pipelines or other industrial infrastructure." Wilderness areas and protected parks are considered important for the survival of certain species, ecological studies, conservation, solitude, and recreation. Wilderness is deeply valued for cultural, spiritual, moral, and aesthetic reasons. Some nature writers believe wilderness areas are vital for the human spirit and creativity.

The word, "wilderness", derives from the notion of wildness; in other words that which is not controllable by humans. The word's etymology is from the Old English wildeornes, which in turn derives from wildeor meaning wild beast (wild + deor = beast, deer). From this point of view, it is the wildness of a place that makes it a wilderness. The mere presence or activity of people does not disqualify an area from being "wilderness." Many ecosystems that are, or have been, inhabited or influenced by activities of people may still be considered "wild." This way of looking at wilderness includes areas within which natural processes operate without very noticeable human interference.

Challenges

It is the common understanding of natural environment that underlies environmentalism — a broad political, social, and philosophical movement that advocates various actions and policies in the interest of protecting what nature remains in the natural environment, or restoring or expanding the role of nature in this environment. While true wilderness is increasingly rare, wild nature (e.g., unmanaged forests, uncultivated grasslands, wildlife, wildflowers) can be found in many locations previously inhabited by humans.

Goals commonly expressed by environmental scientists include:

- Reduction and clean up of pollution, with future goals of zero pollution;
- Cleanly converting nonrecyclable materials into energy through direct combustion or after conversion into secondary fuels;
- Reducing societal consumption of non-renewable fuels;
- Development of alternative, green, low-carbon or renewable energy sources;
- Conservation and sustainable use of scarce resources such as water, land, and air;
- Protection of representative or unique or pristine ecosystems;

- Preservation of threatened and endangered species extinction.

The establishment of nature and biosphere reserves under various types of protection; and, most generally, the protection of biodiversity and ecosystems upon which all human and other life on earth depends.

Very large development projects - megaprojects - pose special challenges and risks to the natural environment. Major dams and power plants are cases in point. The challenge to the environment from such projects is growing because more and bigger megaprojects are being built, in developed and developing nations alike.

BIODIVERSITY

Biodiversity is the variation of life forms within a given ecosystem, biome, or for the entire Earth. Biodiversity is often used as a measure of the health of biological systems. The biodiversity found on Earth today consists of many millions of distinct biological species, which is the product of nearly 3.5 billion years of evolution.

Evolution and Meaning

Biodiversity is a portmanteau word, from biology and diversity, originating from and used interchangeably with "biological diversity." This term was used first by wildlife scientist and conservationist Raymond F. Dasmann in a lay book advocating nature conservation. It was not widely adopted for more than a decade, when in the 1980s it and "biodiversity" came into common usage in science and environmental policy. Use of the term by Thomas Lovejoy in the Forward to the book credited with launching the field of conservation biology introduced the term along with "conservation biology" to the scientific community. Until then the term "natural diversity" was used in conservation science circles, including by The Science Division of The Nature Conservancy in an important 1975 study, "The Preservation of Natural Diversity." By the early 1980s TNC's

Science program and its head Robert E. Jenkins, Lovejoy, and other leading conservation scientists at the time in America advocated the use of "biological diversity" to embrace the object of biological conservation.

Its contracted form biodiversity may have been coined by W.G. Rosen in 1985 while planning the National Forum on Biological Diversity organized by the National Research Council (NRC) which was to be held in 1986, and first appeared in a publication in 1988 when entomologist E. O. Wilson used it as the title of the proceedings of that forum.

Since this period both terms and the concept have achieved widespread use among biologists, environmentalists, political leaders, and concerned citizens worldwide. It is generally used to equate to a concern for the natural environment and nature conservation. This use has coincided with the expansion of concern over extinction observed in the last decades of the 20th century.

A similar concept in use in the United States, besides natural diversity, is the term "natural heritage." It pre-dates both terms though it is a less scientific term and more easily comprehended in some ways by the wider audience interested in conservation. "Natural Heritage" was used when Jimmy Carter set up the Georgia Heritage Trust while he was governor of Georgia; Carter's trust dealt with both natural and cultural heritage. It would appear that Carter picked the term up from Lyndon Johnson, who used it in a 1966 Message to Congress. "Natural Heritage" was picked up by the Science Division of the US Nature Conservancy when, under Jenkins, it launched in 1974 the network of State Natural Heritage Programs. When this network was extended outside the USA, the term "Conservation Data Center" was suggested by Guillermo Mann and came to be preferred.

Definitions

Biologists most often define "biological diversity" or "biodiversity" as the "totality of genes, species, and ecosystems of a region". An advantage of this definition is that it seems to describe most circumstances and present a unified view of the traditional three levels at which biological variety has been identified:

- genetic diversity;
- species diversity; and
- Ecosystem diversity

This multilevel conception is consistent with the early use of "biological diversity in Washington. D.C. and international conservation organizations in the late 1960s through 1970's, by Raymond F. Dasmann who apparently coined the term and Thomas E. Lovejoy who later introduced it to the wider conservation and science communities. An explicit definition consistent with this interpretation was first given in a paper by Bruce A. Wilcox commissioned by The International Union for the Conservation of Nature and Natural Resources (IUCN) for the 1982 World National Parks Conference in Bali. The definition Wilcox gave is "Biological diversity is the variety of life forms ... at all levels of biological systems (i.e., molecular, organismal, population, species and ecosystem)..." Subsequently, the 1992 United Nations Earth Summit in Rio de Janeiro defined "biological diversity" as "the variability among living organisms from all sources, including, 'inter alia', terrestrial, marine, and other aquatic ecosystems, and the ecological complexes of which they are part: this includes diversity within species, between species and of ecosystems". This is, in fact, the closest thing to a single legally accepted definition of biodiversity, since it is the definition adopted by the United Nations Convention on Biological Diversity.

If the gene is the fundamental unit of natural selection, according to E.O. Wilson, the real biodiversity is genetic diversity. For geneticists, biodiversity is the diversity of genes and organisms. They study processes such as mutations, gene exchanges, and genome dynamics that occur at the DNA level and generate evolution. Consistent with this, along with the above definition the Wilcox paper stated "genes are the ultimate source of biological organization at all levels of biological systems..."

Measurement

It has been suggested that some content from this article be split into a separate article entitled Measurement of biodiversity.

Polar bears on the sea ice of the Arctic Ocean, near the north pole.Biodiversity is a broad concept, so a variety of objective measures have been created in order to empirically measure biodiversity. Each measure of biodiversity relates to a particular use of the data.

For practical conservationists, this measure should quantify a value that is broadly shared among locally affected people. For others, a more economically defensible definition should allow the ensuring of continued possibilities for both adaptation and future use by people, assuring environmental sustainability.

As a consequence, biologists argue that this measure is likely to be associated with the variety of genes. Since it cannot always be said which genes are more likely to prove beneficial, the best choice for conservation is to assure the persistence of as many genes as possible. For ecologists, this latter approach is sometimes considered too restrictive, as it prohibits ecological succession.

Biodiversity is usually plotted as taxonomic richness of a geographic area, with some reference to a temporal scale.

Distribution

Selection bias continues to bedevil modern estimates of biodiversity. In 1768 Rev. Gilbert White succinctly observed of his Selborne, Hampshire "all nature is so full, that that district produces the most variety which is the most examined."

Nevertheless, biodiversity is not distributed evenly on Earth. It is consistently richer in the tropics and in other localized regions such as the Cape Floristic Province. As one approaches polar regions one generally finds fewer species. Flora and fauna diversity depends on climate, altitude, soils and the presence of other species. In the year 2006 large numbers of the Earth's species were formally classified as rare or endangered or threatened species; moreover, many scientists have estimated that there are millions more species actually endangered which have not yet been formally recognized. About 40 percent of the 40,177 species assessed using the IUCN Red List criteria, are now listed as threatened species with extinction - a total of 16,119 species.

Even though biodiversity declines from the equator to the poles in terrestrial ecoregions, whether this is so in aquatic ecosystems is still a hypothesis to be tested, especially in marine ecosystems where causes of this phenomenon are unclear In addition, particularly in marine ecosystems, there are several well stated cases where diversity in higher latitudes actually increases. Therefore, the lack of information on biodiversity of Tropics and Polar Regions prevents scientific conclusions on the distribution of the world's aquatic biodiversily.

A biodiversity hotspot is a region with a high level of endemic species. These biodiversity hotspots were first identified by Dr. Norman Myers in two articles in the scientific journal The Environmentalist Dense human habitation tends to occur near hotspots. Most hotspots are located in the tropics and most of them are forests.

Brazil's Atlantic Forest is considered a hotspot of biodiversity and contains roughly 20,000 plant species, 1350 vertebrates, and millions of insects, about half of which occur nowhere else in the world. The island of Madagascar including the unique Madagascar dry deciduous forests and lowland rainforests possess a very high ratio of species endemism and biodiversity, since the island separated from mainland Africa 65 million years ago, most of the species and ecosystems have evolved independently producing unique species different from those in other parts of Africa.

Many regions of high biodiversity (as well as high endemism) arise from very specialized habitats which require unusual adaptation mechanisms. For example the peat bogs of Northern Europe.

Evolution

Biodiversity found on Earth today is the result of 4 billion years of evolution. The origin of life has not been definitely established by science, however some evidence suggests that life may already have been well-established a few hundred million years after the formation of the Earth. Until approximately 600 million years ago, all life consisted of archaea, bacteria, protozoans and similar single-celled organisms.

The history of biodiversity during the Phanerozoic (the last 540 million years), starts with rapid growth during the Cambrian explosion—a period during which nearly every phylum of multicellular organisms first appeared. Over the next 400 million years or so, global diversity showed little overall trend, but was marked by periodic, massive losses of diversity classified as mass extinction events.

The apparent biodiversity shown in the fossil record suggests that the last few million years include the period of greatest biodiversity in the Earth's history. However, not all scientists support this view, since there is considerable uncertainty as to how strongly the fossil record is biased by the greater availability and preservation of recent geologic sections. Some (e.g. Alroy et al. 2001) argue that, corrected for sampling artifacts, modern biodiversity is not much different from biodiversity 300 million years ago. Estimates of the present global macroscopic species diversity vary from 2 million to 100 million species, with a best estimate of somewhere near 13-14 million, the vast majority of them arthropods.

Most biologists agree however that the period since the emergence of humans is part of a new mass extinction, the Holocene extinction event, caused primarily by the impact humans are having on the environment. It has been argued that the present rate of extinction is sufficient to eliminate most species on the planet Earth within 100 years.

New species are regularly discovered (on average between 5-10,000 new species each year, most of them insects) and many, though discovered, are not yet classified (estimates are that nearly 90% of all arthropods are not yet classified). Most of the terrestrial diversity is found in tropical forests.

Human Benefits

There are a multitude of direct anthropocentric benefits of biodiversity in the areas of agriculture, science and medicine, industrial materials, ecological services, in leisure, and in cultural, aesthetic and intellectual value, although biodiversity includes pest species and organisms of no known interest or direct use.

Biodiversity also supports a number of natural ecosystem processes and services. Some ecosystem services that benefit society are air quality, climate (both global CO_2 sequestration and local), water purification, disease control, biological pest control, pollination and prevention of erosion. Biodiversity is also believed to create stability in ecosystems, allowing these ecosystems to continue providing services in the face of disturbances.

Non-material benefits that are obtained from ecosystems include spiritual and aesthetic values, knowledge systems and the value of education. Biodiversity is also central to an ecocentric philosophy.

Agriculture

The economic value of the reservoir of genetic traits present in wild v largely due to harnessing the genetic diversity present in wild and domestic crop plants. Interbreeding crops strains with different beneficial traits has resulted in more than doubling crop prodction in the last 50 years as a result of the Green Revolution.

Crop diversity is also necessary to help the system recover when the dominant crop type is attacked by a disease.

- The Irish potato blight of 1846, which was a major factor in the death of a million people and migration of another million, was the ret of planting only two potato varieties, both of which were vulnerable.
- Wen rice grassy stunt virus struck rice fields from Indonesia to India in the 1970s. 6273 varieties were tested for resistance. One was found to be resistant, an Indian variety, known to science only since 1966This veriety formed a hybrid with other varieties and is now widely grown.
- Coffe rust attacked coffee plantations in Sri Lanka, Brazil, and Central America in 1970. A resistant variety was found in Ethiopia. Although the diseases are themselves a form of biodiversity.

Monlture, the lack of biodiversity, was a contributing factor to several agricultural disasters in history, including the Irish Potato Famine, the European wine industry collapse in the late 1800s, and the US Southern Corn Leaf Blight epidemic of 1970.

Higher biodiversity also controls the spread of certain diseases as pathogens will need to adapt to infect different species.

Amazon Rainforest in Brazil.Biodiversity provides food for humans. Although about 80 percent of our food supply comes from just 20 kinds of plants, humans use at least 40,000 species of plant and animals a day. Many people around the world depend on hese species for their food, shelter, and clothing. There is untapped potential for increasing the range of food products suitable for human consumption, provided that the high present extinction rate can be stopped.

SCIENCE AND MEDICINE

A significant proportion of drugs are derived, directly or indirectly, from biological sources; in most cases these medicines can not presently be synthesized in a laboratory setting. About 40% of the pharmaceuticals used in the US are manufactured using natural compounds found in plants, animals, and microorganisms. Moreover, only a small proportion of the total diversity of plants has been thoroughly investigated for potential sources of new drugs. Many drugs are also derived from microorganisms, although in many cases these drugs have the purpose of attacking other micro-organisms which humans would benefit from eradicating.

Through the field of bionics, considerable technological advancement has occurred which would not have without a rich biodiversity.

Industrial Materials

A wide range of industrial materials are derived directly from biological resources. These include building materials, fibers, dyes, resirubber and oil. There is enormous potential for further research into sustainably utilizing materials from a wider diversity of organisms.

Biodiversity provides many ecosystem services that are often not readily visible. It plays a part in regulating the chemistry of our atmosphere and water supply. Biodiversity is directly involved in water purification, recycling nutrients and providing fertile soils. Experiments with controlled environments have shown that humans cannot easily build ecosystems to support human needs; for example insect pollination cannot be mimicked by human-made construction, and that activity alone represents tens of billions of dollars in ecosystem services per annum to humankind.

The stability of ecosystems is also related to biodiversity, with higher biodiversity producing greater stability over time, reducing the chance that ecosystem services will be disrupted as a result of disturbances such as extreme weather events or human exploitation.

Leisure, Cultural and Aesthetic Value

Many people derive value from biodiversity through leisure activities such as hiking, birdwatching or natural history study. Biodiversity has inspired musicians, painters, sculptors, writers and other artists. Many cultural groups view themselves as an integral part of the natural world and show respect for other living organisms.

Popular activities such as gardening, caring for aquariums and collecting butterflies are all strongly dependent on biodiversity. The number of species involved in such pursuits is in the tens of thousands, though the great majority do not enter mainstream commercialism.

The relationships between the original natural areas of these often 'exotic' animals and plants and commercial collectors, suppliers, breeders, propagators and those who promote their understanding and enjoyment are complex and poorly understood. It seems clear, however, that the general public responds well to exposure to rare and unusual organisms—they recognize their inherent value at some level. A family outing to the botanical garden or zoo is as much an aesthetic or cultural experience as it is an educational one.

Philosophically it could be argued that biodiversity has intrinsic aesthetic and spiritual value to mankind in and of itself. This idea can be used as a counterweight to the notion that tropical forests and other ecological realms are only worthy of conservation because they may contain medicines or useful products.

An interesting point is that evolved DNA embodies knowledge and therefore destroying a species resembles burning a book, with the caveat that the book is of uncertain depth and importance and may in fact be best used as fuel.

Threats to Biodiversity

During the last century, erosion of biodiversity has been increasingly observed. Some studies show that about one eighth known plant species is threatened with extinction Some estimates put the loss at up to 140,000 species per year (based on Species-area theory) and subject to discussion This figure indicates unsustainable ecological practices, because only a small number of species come into being each year. Almost all scientists acknowledge that the rate of species loss is greater now than at any time in human history, with extinctions occurring at rates hundreds of times higher than background extinction rates.

The factors that threaten biodiversity have been variously categorized. Jared Diamond describes an "Evil Quartet" of habitat destruction, overkill, introduced species, and secondary extensions. Edward O. Wilson prefers the acronym HIPPO, standing for Habitat destruction, Invasive species, Pollution, Human OverPopulation, and Overharvesting. The most authoritative classification in use today is that of IUCN's Classification of Direct Threats adopted by most major international conservation organizations such as the US Nature Conservancy, the World Wildlife Fund, Conservation International, and Birdlife International.

Destruction of Habitat

Most of the species extinctions from 1000 AD to 2000 AD are due to human activities, in particular destruction of plant and animal habitats. Raised rates of extinction are being driven by human consumption of organic resources, especially related to tropical forest destruction. While most of the species that are becoming extinct are not food species, their biomass is converted into human food when their habitat is transformed into pasture, cropland, and orchards. It is estimated that more than a third of the Earth's biomass is tied up in only the few species that represent humans, livestock and crops. Because an ecosystem decreases in stability as its species are made extinct, these studies warn that the global ecosystem is destined for collapse if it is further reduced in complexity. Factors contributing to loss of biodiversity are: overpopulation, deforestation, pollution (air pollution, water pollution, soil contamination) and global warming or climate change, driven by human activity. These factors, while all stemming from overpopulation, produce a cumulative impact upon biodiversity.

There are systematic relationships between the area of a habitat and the number of species it can support, with greater sensitivity to reduction in habitat area for species of larger body size and for those living at lower latitudes or in forests or oceans Some characterize loss of biodiversity not as ecosystem degradation but by conversion to trivial standardized ecosystems (e.g., monoculture following deforestation). In some countries lack of property rights or access regulation to biotic resources necessarily leads to biodiversity loss (degradation costs having to be supported by the community).

A September 14, 2007 study conducted by the National Science Foundation found that biodiversity and genetic diversity are dependent upon each other—that diversity within a species is necessary to maintain diversity among species, and vice versa. According to the lead researcher in the study, Dr. Richard Lankau, "If any one type is removed from the system, the cycle can break down, and the community becomes dominated by a single species."

At present, the most threathened ecosystems are those found in fresh water. The marking of fresh water ecosystems as the ecosystems most under threat was done by the Millennium Ecosystem Assessment 2005, and was confirmed again by the project "Freshwater Animal Diversity Assessment", organised by the biodiversity platform, and the French Institut de recherche pour le développement (MNHNP)

Exotic Species

The rich diversity of unique species across many parts of the world exist only because they are separated by barriers, particularly large rivers, seas, oceans, mountains and deserts from other species of other land masses, particularly the highly fecund, ultra-competitive, generalist "super-species". These are barriers that couldn't have be easily crossed by natural processes, except through continental drift. However humans have invented transportation with the ability to bring into contact species that never have met in their evolutionary history, and on a time scale of days, unlike the centuries that historically have accompanied major animal migrations.

The widespread introduction of exotic species by humans is a potent threat to biodiversity. When exotic species are introduced to ecosystems and establish self-sustaining populations, the endemic species in that ecosystem that have not evolved to cope with the exotic species may not survive. The exotic organisms may be either predators, parasites, or simply aggressive species that deprive indigenous species of nutrients, water and light. These invasive species often have features, due to their evolutionary background and new environment, that make them highly competitive; able to become well-established and spread quickly, reducing the effective habitat of endemic species.

As a consequence of the above, if humans continue to combine species from different ecoregions, there is the potential that the world's ecosystems will end up dominated by relatively a few, aggressive, cosmopolitan "super-species". In 2004, an international team of scientists estimated that 10 percent of species would become extinct by 2050 because of global warming

"We need to limit climate change or we wind up with a lot of species in trouble, possibly extinct," said Dr. Lee Hannah, a co-author of the paper and chief climate change biologist at the Center for Applied Biodiversity Science at Conservation International.

Genetic Pollution

Purebred naturally evolved region specific wild species can be threatened with extinction through the process of genetic pollution i.e. uncontrolled hybridization, introgression and genetic swamping which leads to homogenization or replacement of local genotypes as a result of either a numerical and/or fitness advantage of introduced plant or animal Nonnative species can bring about a form of extinction of native plants and animals by hybridization and introgression either through purposeful introduction by humans or through habitat modification, bringing previously isolated species into contact. These phenomena can be especially detrimental for rare species coming into contact with more abundant ones. The abundant species can interbreed with the rarer, swamping the entire gene pool and creating hybrids, thus driving the entire native stock to complete extinction. Attention has to be focused on the extent of this under appreciated problem that is not always apparent from morphological (outward appearance) observations alone. Some degree of gene flow may be a normal, evolutionarily constructive, process, and all constellations of genes and genotypes cannot be preserved. However, hybridization with or without introgression may, nevertheless, threaten a rare species' existence

Hybridization and Genetics

In agriculture and animal husbandry, the green revolution popularized the use of conventional hybridization to increase yield by creating "high-yielding varieties". Often the handful of hybridized breeds originated in developed countries and were further hybridized with local varieties in the rest of the developing world to create high yield strains resistant to local climate and diseases. Local governments and industry have been pushing hybridization which has resulted in several of the indigenous breeds becoming extinct or threatened. Disuse because of unprofitability and uncontrolled intentional and unintentional cross-pollination and crossbreeding (genetic pollution), formerly huge gene pools of various wild and indigenous breeds have collapsed causing widespread genetic erosion and genetic pollution. This has resulted in loss of genetic diversity and biodiversity as a whole.

A genetically modified organism (GMO) is an organism whose genetic material has been altered using the genetic engineering techniques generally known as recombinant DNA technology. Genetically Modified (GM) crops today have become a common source for genetic pollution, not only of wild varieties but also of other domesticated varieties derived from relatively natural hybridization.

Genetic erosion coupled with genetic pollution may be destroying unique genotypes, thereby creating a hidden crisis which could result in a severe threat to our food security. Diverse genetic material could cease to exist which would impact our ability to further hybridize food crops and livestock against more resistant diseases and climatic changes.

Conserving Biodiversity

A schematic image illustrating the relationship between biodiversity, ecosystem services, human well-being, and poverty The illustration shows where conservation action, strategies and plans can influence the drivers of the current biodiversity crisis at local, regional, to global scales.Conservation biology matured in the mid- 20th century as ecologists, naturalists, and other scientists began to collectively research and address issues pertaining to global declines in biodiversity.The conservation ethic differs from the preservationist ethic, historically lead by John Muir, who advocate for protected areas devoid of human exploitation or interference for profitThe conservation ethic advocates for wise stewardship and management of natural resource production for the purpose of protecting and sustaining biodiversity in species, ecosystems, the evolutionary process, and human culture and society Conservation biologists are concerned with the trends in biodiversity being reported in this era, which has been labeled by science as the Holocene extinction period, also known as the sixth mass extinction Rates of decline in biodiversity in this sixth mass extinction exceeds the five previous extinction spasms recorded in the fossil record. In response to the extinction crisis, the research of conservation biologists is being organized into strategic plans that include principles, guidelines, and tools for the purpose of protecting biodiversity. Conservation biology is a crisis orientated discipline and it is multi-disciplinary, including ecological, social, education, and other scientific disciplines outside of biology. Conservation biologists work in both the field and office, in government, universities, non-profit organizations and in industry. The conservation of biological diversity is a global priority in strategic conservation plans that are designed to engage public policy and concerns affecting local, regional and global scales of communities, ecosystems, and cultures Conserving biodiversity and action plans identify ways of sustaining human well-being and global economics, including natural capital, market capital, and ecosystem services.

Judicial Status

Biodiversity is beginning to be evaluated and its evolution analysed (through observations, inventories, conservation...) as well as being taken into account in political and judicial decisions.

- The relationship between law and ecosystems is very ancient and has consequences for biodiversity. It is related to property rights, both private and public. It can define protection for threatened ecosystems, but also some rights and duties (for example, fishing rights, hunting rights).
- Law regarding species is a more recent issue. It defines species that must be protected because they may be threatened by extinction. The U.S. Endangered Species Act is an example of an attempt to address the "law and species" issue.
- Laws regarding gene pools are only about a century old While the genetic approach is not new (domestication, plant traditional selection methods), progress made in the genetic field in the past 20 years have led to a tightening of laws in this field. With the new technologies of genetic analysis and genetic engineering, people are going through gene patenting, processes patenting, and a totally new concept of genetic resources. A very hot debate today seeks to define whether the resource is the gene, the organism itself, or its DNA.

The 1972 UNESCO convention established that biological resources, such as plants, were the common heritage of mankind. These rules probably inspired the creation of great public banks of genetic resources, located outside the source-countries.

New global agreements (e.g. Convention on Biological Diversity), now give sovereign national rights over biological resources (not property). The idea of static conservation of biodiversity is disappearing and being replaced by the idea of dynamic conservation, through the notion of resource and innovation.

The new agreements commit countries to conserve biodiversity, develop resources for sustainability and share the benefits resulting from their use. Under new rules, it is expected that bioprospecting or collection of natural products has to be allowed by the biodiversity-rich country, in exchange for a share of the benefits.

Sovereignty principles can rely upon what is better known as Access and Benefit Sharing Agreements (ABAs). The Convention on Biodiversity spirit implies a prior informed consent between the source country and the collector, to establish which resource will be used and for what, and to settle on a fair agreement on benefit sharing. Bioprospecting can become a type of biopiracy when those principles are not respected.

Uniform approval for use of biodiversity as a legal standard has not been achieved, however. At least one legal commentator has argued that biodiversity should not be used as a legal standard, arguing that the multiple layers of scientific uncertainty inherent in the concept of biodiversity will cause administrative waste and increase litigation without promoting preservation goals.

Analytical Limits

Taxonomic and Size Bias

Less than 1% of all species that have been described have been studied beyond simply noting its existence. Biodiversity researcher Sean Nee points out that the vast majority of Earth's biodiversity is microbial, and that contemporary biodiversity physics is "firmly fixated on the visible world" (Nee uses "visible" as a synonym for macroscopic) For example, microbial life is very much more metabolically and environmentally diverse than multicellular life Nee has stated: "On the tree of life, based on analyses of small-subunit ribosomal RNA, visible life consists of barely noticeable twigs.

The size bias is not restricted to consideration of microbes. Entomologist Nigel Stork states that "to a first approximation, all multicellular species on Earth are insects". Even in insects, however, the extinction rate is high and indicative of the general trend of the sixth greatest extinction period that human society is faced with. Moreover, there are species co-extinctions, such as plants and beetles, where the extinction or decline in one is reciprocated in the other.

Definition of Biodiversity

1. Biodiversity is the variety of life: the different plants, animals and micro-organisms, their genes and the ecosystems of which they are a part. It is home to more than one million species of plants and animals, many of which are found nowhere else in the world.

2. "Biodiversity" is often defined as the variety of all forms of life, from genes to species, through to the broad scale of ecosystems (for a list of variants on this simple definition see Gaston 1996). "Biodiversity" was coined as a contraction of "biological diversity" in 1985, but the new term arguably has taken on a meaning and import all its own. A symposium in 1986, and the follow-up book Biodiversity (Wilson 1988), edited by biologist E. O. Wilson, heralded the popularity of this concept. Ten years later, Takacs (1996, p. 39) described its ascent this way: "in 1988, biodiversity did not appear as a keyword in Biological Abstracts, and biological diversity appeared once. In 1993, biodiversity appeared seventy-two times, and biological diversity nineteen times". Fifteen years further on, it would be hard to count how many times "biodiversity" is used every day by scientists, policy-makers, and others. The global importance of biodiversity now is reflected in the widely accepted target to achieve a significant reduction in the rate of loss of biodiversity by the year 2010.

11

ENVIRONMENTALISM

Environmentalism is a broad philosophy and social movement centered on a concern for the conservation and improvement of the environment. Environmentalism is associated with the colour green.

Environmentalism as a Social Movement

Environmentalism can also be defined as a social movement which seeks to influence the political process by lobbying, activism, and education in order to protect natural resources and ecosystems. In recognition of humanity as a participant in ecosystems, the environmental movement is centered on ecology, health, and human rights.

An environmentalist is a person who may advocate the sustainable management of resources and stewardship of the natural environment through changes in public policy or individual behavior. In various ways (for example, grassroots activism and protests), environmentalists and environmental organizations seek to give the natural world a stronger voice in human affairs.

History

Though the modern environmental movement arose during the Industrial Revolution a concern for environmental protection has recurred in diverse forms, in different parts of the world, throughout history. For example, in the Middle East, the earliest known writings concerned with environmental pollution were Arabic medical treatises written during the "Arab Agricultural Revolution", by writers such as Alkindus, Costa ben Luca, Rhazes, Ibn Al-Jazzar, al-Tamimi, al-Masihi, Avicenna, Ali ibn Ridwan, Isaac Israeli ben Solomon, Abd-el-latif, and Ibn al-Nafis. They were concerned with air contamination, water contamination, soil contamination, solid waste mishandling, and environmental assessments of certain localities.

In Europe, King Edward I of England banned the burning of sea-coal by proclamation in London in 1272, after its smoke had become a problem But the fuel was so common in England that this earliest of names for it was acquired because it could be carted away from some shores by the wheelbarrow. Air pollution would continue to be a problem there, especially later during the industrial revolution, and extending into the recent past with the Great Smog of 1952.

Origins of Environmental Movement

In Europe, it was the Industrial Revolution that gave rise to modern environmental pollution as it is generally understood today. The emergence of great factories and consumption of immense quantities of coal and other fossil fuels gave rise to unprecedented air pollution and the large volume of industrial chemical discharges added to the growing load of untreated human waste The first large-scale, modern environmental laws came in the form of the British Alkali Acts, passed in 1863, to regulate the deleterious air pollution (gaseous hydrochloric acid) given off by the Leblanc process, used to produce soda ash. Environmentalism grew out of the amenity movement, which was a reaction to industrialization, the growth of cities, and worsening air and water pollution.

In the United States, the beginnings of an environmental movement can be traced as far back as 1739, when Benjamin Franklin and other Philadelphia residents, citing "public rights," petitioned the Pennsylvania Assembly to stop waste dumping and remove tanneries from Philadelphia's commercial district. The US movement expanded in the 1800s, out of concerns for protecting the natural resources of the West, with individuals such as John Muir and Henry David Thoreau making key philosophical contributions. Thoreau was interested in peoples' relationship with nature and studied this by living close to nature in a simple life. He published his experiences in the book Walden, which argues that people should become intimately close with nature. Muir came to believe in nature's inherent right, especially after spending time hiking in Yosemite Valley and studying both the ecology and geology. He successfully lobbied congress to form Yosemite National Park and went on to set up the Sierra Club. The conservationist principles as well as the belief in an inherent right of nature were to become the bedrock of modern environmentalism.

In the 20th century, environmental ideas continued to grow in popularity and recognition. Efforts were starting to be made to save some wildlife, particularly the American Bison. The death of the last Passenger Pigeon as well as the endangerment of the American Bison helped to focus the minds of conservationists and popularize their concerns. Notably in 1916 the National Park Service was founded by President Woodrow Wilson.

In 1949, A Sand County Almanac by Aldo Leopold was published. It explained Leopold's belief that humankind should have moral respect for the environment and that it is unethical to harm it. The book is sometimes called the most influential book on conservation.

In 1962, Houghton Mifflin published *Silent Spring* by American biologist Rachel Carson. The book catalogued the environmental impacts of the indiscriminate spraying of DDT in the US and questioned the logic of releasing large amounts of chemicals into the environment without fully understanding their effects on ecology or human health. The book suggested that DDT and other pesticides may cause cancer and that their agricultural use was a threat to wildlife, particularly birds. The resulting public concern lead to the creation of the United States Environmental Protection Agency in 1970 which subsequently banned the agricultural use of DDT in the US in 1972. The limited use of DDT in disease vector control continues to this day in certain parts of the world and remains controversial. The book's legacy was to produce a far greater awareness of environmental issues and interest into how people affect the environment. With this new interest in environment came interest in problems such as air pollution and oil spills, and environmental interest grew. New pressure groups formed, notably Greenpeace and Friends of the Earth.

In the 1970s, the Chipko movement was formed in India; influenced by Mahatma Gandhi, they set up peaceful resistance to deforestation by literally hugging trees (leading to the term "tree huggers"). Their peaceful methods of protest and slogan "ecology is permanent economy" were very influential.

By the mid-1970s, many felt that people were on the edge of environmental catastrophe. The Back-to-the-land movement started to form and ideas of environmental ethics joined with anti-Vietnam War sentiments and other political issues. These individuals lived outside normal society and started to take on some of the more radical environmental theories such as deep ecology. Around this time more mainstream environmentalism was starting to show force with the signing of the Endangered Species Act in 1973 and the formation of CITES in 1975.

In 1979, James Lovelock, a former NASA scientist, published Gaia: A new look at life on Earth, which put forth the Gaia Hypothesis; it proposes that life on Earth can be understood as a single organism. This became an important part of the Deep Green ideology. Throughout the rest of the history of environmentalism there has been debate and argument between more radical followers of this Deep Green ideology and more mainstream environmentalists.

Environmentalism has also changed to deal with new issues such as *global warming* and *genetic engineering*.

Environmental Movement

The environmental movement (a term that sometimes includes the conservation and green movements) is a diverse scientific, social, and political movement. In general terms, environmentalists advocate the sustainable management of resources, and the protection (and restoration, when necessary) of the natural environment through changes in public policy and individual behavior. In its recognition of humanity as a participant in ecosystems, the movement is centered around ecology, health, and human rights. Additionally, throughout history, the movement has been incorporated into religion. The movement is represented by a range of organizations, from the large to grassroots, but a younger demographic than is common in other social movements. Due to its large membership, varying and strong beliefs, the movement is not entirely united. Indeed, some argue that an environmental ethic of at least some sort is so urgently needed in all quarters that the broader the better. Conversely, disunity can be a weakness in the face of strong opposition from unsympathetic political and industrial forces.

Free Market Environmentalism

Free market environmentalism is a theory that argues that the free market, property rights, and tort law provide the best tools to preserve the health and sustainability of the environment. This is in sharp contrast to the most common approach of looking to legislative government intervention to prevent destruction of the environment. It considers environmental stewardship to be natural, as well as the expulsion of pollutors and other aggressors through individual and class action.

Preservation and Conservation

Environmental preservation, chiefly in the United States, is viewed as the strict setting aside of natural resources to prevent damage caused by contact with humans or by certain human activities, such as logging, mining, hunting, and fishing. It is different from conservation; conservation allows for some degree of industrial development, albeit it within sustainable limits. Regulations and laws may be enacted for the preservation of natural resources.

Elsewhere in the world the terms preservation and conservation may be less contested and are often used interchangeably.

Dark Greens, Light Greens and Bright Greens

Contemporary environmentalists are often described as being split into three groups: Dark, Light, and Bright Greens.

- Light Greens see protecting the environment first and foremost as a personal responsibility. They fall in on the reformist end of the spectrum introduced above, but light Greens do not emphasize environmentalism as a distinct political ideology, or even seek fundamental political reform. Instead they often focus on environmentalism as a lifestyle choiceThe motto "Green is the new black." sums up this way of thinking.
- In contrast, Dark Greens believe that environmental problems are an inherent part of industrialized capitalism, and seek radical political change. As discussed earlier, 'dark greens' tend to believe that dominant political ideologies (sometimes referred to as industrialism) are corrupt and inevitably lead to consumerism, alienation from nature and resource

depletion. Dark Greens claim that this is caused by the emphasis on growth that exists within all existing ideologies, a tendency referred to as 'growth mania'. The dark green brand of environmentalism is associated with ideas of Deep Ecology, Post-materialism, Holism, the Gaia Theory of James Lovelock and the work of Fritjof Capra. The division between light and dark greens was visible in the fighting between Fundi and Realo factions of the German Green Party. Since the Dark Greens often embrace strands of communist and marxist philosophies, the motto "Green is the new red." is often used in describing their beliefs.

- More recently, a third group may be said to have emerged in the form of Bright Greens. This group believes that radical changes are needed in the economic and political operation of society in order to make it sustainable, but that better designs, new technologies and more widely distributed social innovations are the means to make those changes— and that we can neither shop nor protest our way to sustainability As Ross Robertson writes, "Right green environmentalism is less about the problems and limitations we need to overcome than the "tools, models, and ideas" that already exist for overcoming them. It forgoes the bleakness of protest and dissent for the energizing confidence of constructive solutions.

Environmental Organizations and Conferences

Environmental organizations can be global, regional, national or local; they can be government-run or private (NGO). Despite a tendency to see environmentalism as an American or Western-centered pursuit, almost every country has its share of environmental activism. Moreover, groups dedicated to community development and social justice may also attend to environmental concerns.

There are some volunteer organisations. For example Ecoworld, which is about the environment and is based in team work and volunteer work. Some US environmental organizations, among them the Natural Resources Defense Council and the Environmental Defense Fund, specialize in bringing lawsuits (a tactic seen as particularly useful in that country). Other groups, such as the US-based National Wildlife Federation, the Nature Conservancy, and The Wilderness Society, and global groups like the World Wide Fund for Nature and Friends of the Earth, disseminate information, participate in public hearings, lobby, stage demonstrations, and may purchase land for preservation. Smaller groups, including Wildlife Conservation International, conduct research on endangered species and ecosystems. More radical organizations, such as Greenpeace, Earth First!, and the Earth Liberation Front, have more directly opposed actions they regard as environmentally harmful. While Greenpeace is devoted to nonviolent confrontation as a means of bearing witness to environmental wrongs and bringing issues into the public realm for debate, the underground Earth Liberation Front engages in the clandestine destruction of property, the release of caged or penned animals, and other criminal acts. Such tactics are regarded as unusual within the movement, however.

On an international level, concern for the environment was the subject of a UN conference in Stockholm in 1972, attended by 114 nations. Out of this meeting developed UNEP (United Nations Environment Programme) and the follow-up United Nations Conference on Environment and Development in 1992. Other international organizations in support of environmental policies development include the Commission for Environmental Cooperation (NAFTA), the European Environment Agency (EEA), and the Intergovernmental Panel on Climate Change (IPCC).

SOIL CONSERVATION

Soil conservation is a set of management strategies for prevention of soil being eroded from the earth's surface or becoming chemically altered by overuse, salinization, acidification, or other chemical soil contamination.

Principle Approaches

The principal approaches these strategies take are:

- choice of vegetative cover;
- erosion prevention;
- salinity management;
- acidity control;
- encouraging health of beneficial soil organisms;
- prevention and remediation of soil contamination; and
- mineralization.

Other ways are:

- no till farming;
- contour plowing;
- wind rows;
- crop rotation;
- the use of natural and man-made fertilizer;
- resting the land.

Many scientific disciplines are involved in these pursuits, including agronomy, hydrology, soil science, meteorology, microbiology, and environmental chemistry.

Crops and Conservation

Decisions regarding appropriate crop rotation, cover crops, and planted windbreaks are central to the ability of surface soils to retain their integrity, both with respect to erosive forces and chemical change from nutrient depletion. Crop rotation is simply the conventional alternation of crops on a given field, so that nutrient depletion is avoided from repetitive chemical uptake/deposition of single crop growth.

Cover crops serve the function of protecting the soil from erosion, weed establishment or excess evapotranspiration; however, they may also serve vital soil chemistry functions. For example, legumes can be ploughed under to augment soil nitrates, and other plants have the ability to metabolize soil contaminants or alter adverse pH. The cover crop Mucuna pruriens (velvet bean) has been used in Nigeria to increase phosphorus availability after application of rock phosphate. Some of these same precepts are applicable to urban landscaping, especially with respect to ground-cover selection for erosion control and weed suppression.

Windbreaks

Windbreaks are created by planting sufficiently dense rows or stands of trees at the windward exposure of an agricultural field subject to wind erosion. Evergreen species are preferred to achieve year-round protection; however, as long as foliage is present in the seasons of bare soil surfaces, the effect of deciduous trees may also be adequate. Trees, shrubs and groundcovers are also effective perimeter treatment for soil erosion prevention, by insuring any surface flows are impeded. A special form of this perimeter or inter-row treatment is the use of a "grassway" that both channels and dissipates runoff through surface friction, impeding surface runoff, and encouraging infiltration of the slowed surface water.

Erosion Prevention

When surface planting is not feasible, there are a variety of mechanical management tactics to protect surface soils from water and wind erosion. Need for these tools arises on construction sites and other situations of transition, where bare soils are exposed. The primary tactics applied are mulching of soil surfaces and use of surface runoff barriers. From 1990 to 2005 considerable innovation has occurred in manufacture of plastic confined hay-bale products, so that a variety of shapes and sizes of runoff barriers can be delivered to the construction site.

There are also conventional practices that farmers have invoked for centuries. These fall into two main categories: contour farming and terracing, standard methods recommended by the U.S. Natural Resources Conservation Service , whose Code 330 is the common standard. Contour farming was practiced by the ancient Phoenicians, and is known to be effective for slopes between two and ten percent . Contour plowing can increase crop yields from 10 to 50 percent, partially as a result from greater soil retention.

There are many erosion control methods that can be used such as conservation tillage systems and crop rotation.

Terraced potato farming on Taquile Island, Peru. Keyline design is an enhancement of contour farming, where the total watershed properties are taken into account in forming the contour lines. Terracing is the practice of creating benches or nearly level layers on a hillside setting. Terraced farming is more common on small farms and in underdeveloped countries, since mechanized equipment is difficult to deploy in this setting.

Human overpopulation is leading to destruction of tropical forests due to widening practices of slash-and-burn and other methods of subsistence farming necessitated by famines in lesser developed countries. A sequel to the deforestation is typically large scale erosion, loss of soil nutrients and sometimes total desertification.

Salinity Management

The ions responsible for salination are: Na^+, K^+, Ca^{2+}, Mg^{2+} and Cl^-. Salinity is estimated to affect about one third of all the earth's arable land. Soil salinity adversely affects the metabolism of most crops, and erosion effects usually follow vegetation failure. Salinity occurs on drylands from overirrigation and in areas with shallow saline water tables. In the case of over-irrigation, salts are deposited in upper soil layers as a byproduct of most soil infiltration; excessive irrigation merely increases the rate of salt deposition. The best-known case of shallow saline water table capillary action occurred in Egypt after the 1970 construction of the Aswan Dam. The change in the groundwater level due to dam construction led to high concentration of salts in the water table. After the construction, the continuous high level of the water table led to soil salination of previously arable land.

Use of humic acids may prevent excess salination, especially in locales where excessive irrigation was practiced. The mechanism involved is that humic acids can fix both anions and cations and eliminate them from root zones. In some cases it may be valuable to find plants that can tolerate saline conditions to use as surface cover until salinity can be reduced; there are a number of such saline-tolerant plants, such as saltbush, a plant found in much of North America and in the Mediterranean regions of Europe.

Soil Per cent Hydrogen (pH)

Soil pH levels adverse to crop growth can occur naturally in some regions; it can also be induced by acid rain or soil contamination from acids or bases. The role of soil pH is to control nutrient availability to vegetation. The principal macronutrients (calcium, phosphorus, nitrogen, potassium, magnesium, sulfur) prefer neutral to slightly alkaline soils. Calcium, magnesium and potassium are usually made available to plants via cation exchange surfaces of organic material and clay soil surface particles. While acidification increases the initial availability of these cations, the residual soil moisture concentrations of nutrient cations can fall to alarmingly low levels after initial nutrient uptake. Moreover, there is no simple relationship of pH to nutrient availability because of the complex combination of soil types, soil moisture regimes and meteorological factors.

The important observation is that pH is the regulatory mechanism to plant nutrient uptake, and that the theoretical concentration of soil nutrients is meaningless until pH levels are in the optimum range for uptake. Soil pH can be raised by amendment by agricultural lime and liming (soil); The pH of an alkaline soil is lowered by adding sulfur, iron sulfate or aluminium sulfate, although these tend to provide costly short term benefits. Urea, urea phosphate, ammonium nitrate, ammonium phosphates, ammonium sulfate and monopotassium phosphate also reduce soil pH.

Soil Organisms

Promoting the viability of beneficial soil organisms is an element of soil conservation; moreover this includes macroscopic species, notably the earthworm, as well as microorganisms. Positive effects of the earthworm are known well, as to aeration and promotion of macronutrient availability. When worms excrete egesta in the form of casts, a balanced selection of minerals and plant nutrients is made into a form accessible for root uptake. US research shows that earthworm casts are five times richer in available nitrogen, seven times richer in available phosphates and eleven times richer in available potash than the surrounding upper150 mm of soil. The weight of casts produced may be greater than 4.5 kg per worm per year. By burrowing, the earthworm is of value in creating soil porosity, creating channels enhancing the processes of aeration and drainage

Micro-organisms

Soil microorganisms play a vital role in macronutrient wildlife. For example, nitrogen fixation is carried out by free-living or symbiotic bacteria. These bacteria have the nitrogenase enzyme that combines gaseous nitrogen with hydrogen to produce ammonia, which is then further converted by the bacteria to make other organic compounds. Some nitrogen fixing bacteria such as rhizobia live in the root nodules of legumes. Here they form a mutualistic relationship with the plant, producing ammonia in exchange for carbohydrates. In the case of the carbon cycle, carbon is transferred within the biosphere as heterotrophs feed on other organisms. This process includes the uptake of dead organic material (detritus) by fungi and bacteria in the form of fermentation or decay phenomena.

Mycorrhizae

Mycorrhizae are symbiotic associations between soil-dwelling fungi and the roots of vascular plants. The mycorrhizal fungi increase the availability of minerals, water, and organic nutrients to the plant, while extracting sugars and amino acids from the plant. There are two main types, endomycorrhizae (which penetrate the roots) and ectomycorrhizae (which resemble 'socks', forming a sheath around the roots). They were discovered when scientists observed that certain seedlings failed to grow or prosper without soil from their native environment.

Some soil microorganisms known as extremophiles have remarkable properties of adaptation to extreme environmental conditions including temperature, pH and water deprivation.

Degradation and Contamination

The viability of soil organisms can be compromised when insecticides and herbicides are applied to planting regimes. Often there are unforeseen and unintended consequences of such chemical use in the form of death of impaired functioning of soil organisms. Thus any use of pesticides should only be undertaken after thorough understanding of residual toxicities upon soil organisms as well as terrestrial ecological components.

Killing soil microorganisms is a deleterious impact of slash and burn agricultural methods. With the surface temperatures generated, virtual annilation of soil and vegetative cover organisms are destroyed, and in many environments these effects can be virtually irreversible (at least for generations of mankind). Shifting cultivation is also a farming system that often employs slash and burn as one of its elements.

Systems, most of which have an adverse effect upon soil quality and plant metabolism. While the role of pH has been discussed above, heavy metals, solvents, petroleum hydrocarbons, herbicides and pesticides also contribute soil residues that are of potential concern. Some of these chemicals are totally extraneous to the agricultural landscape, but others (notably herbicides and pesticides) are intentionally introduced to serve a short term function. Many of these added chemicals have long half-lives in soil, and others degrade to produce derivative chemicals that may be either persistent or pernicious.

Typically the expense of soil contamination remediation cannot be justified in an agricultural economic analysis, since cleanup costs are generally quite high; often remediation is mandated by state and county environmental health agencies based upon human health risk issues.

Mineralization

To allow plants full realization of their phytonutrient potential, active mineralization of the soil is sometimes undertaken. This can be in the natural form of adding crushed rock or can take the form of chemical soil supplement. In either case the purpose is to combat mineral depletion of the soil. There are a broad range of minerals that can be added including common substances such as phosphorus and more exotic substances such as zinc and selenium. There is extensive research on the phase transitions of minerals in soil with aqueous contact.

The process of flooding can bring significant bedload sediment to an alluvial plain. While this effect may not be desirable if floods endanger life or if the eroded sediment originates from productive land, this process of addition to a floodplain is a natural process that can rejuvenate soil chemistry through mineralization and macronutrient addition.

12

NATURAL RESOURCE

Natural resources (economically referred to as land or raw materials) are naturally forming substances that are considered valuable in their relatively unmodified (natural) form. A natural resource's value rests in the amount and extractability of the material available and the demand for it. The latter is determined by its usefulness to production. A commodity is generally considered a natural resource when the primary activities associated with it are extraction and purification, as opposed to creation. Thus, mining, petroleum extraction, fishing, hunting, and forestry are generally considered natural-resource industries, while agriculture is not. The term was introduced to a broad audience by E.F. Schumacher in his 1970s book Small is Beautiful The term is defined by the United States Geological Survey as "The Nation's natural resources include its minerals, energy, land, water, and biota.

Classification of Natural Forms

Natural resources are mostly classified into renewable and non-renewable resources. Sometimes resources are classified as non-renewable even if they are technically renewable, just not easily renewed within a reasonable amount of time, such as fossil fuels.

Renewable Resources

A natural resource qualifies as a renewable resource if it is replenished by natural processes at a rate comparable or faster than its rate of consumption by humans. Solar radiation, tides, winds and hydroelectricity are perpetual resources that are in no danger of long-term availability. Renewable resources may also mean commodities such as wood, paper, and leather, if harvesting is performed in a sustainable manner.

Some natural renewable resources such as geothermal power, fresh water, timber, and biomass must be carefully managed to avoid exceeding the environment's capacity to replenish them. A life cycle assessment provides a systematic means of evaluating renewability.

The term has a connotation of sustainability of the natural environment. Gasoline, coal, natural gas, diesel, and other commodities derived from fossil fuels are non-renewable. Unlike fossil fuels, a renewable resource can have a sustainable yield.

Renewable resources are sometimes living resources,(trees and soil, for example), which can restock (renew) themselves if used sustainably and not over-harvested. There are also non-living resources that are renewable, such as hydroelectric power, solar power, biomass fuel, and wind power. If renewable resources are consumed at a rate above their natural rate of replacement, the standing stock will diminish and eventually run out. The rate of sustainable use of a renewable resource is determined by the replacement rate and amount of standing stock of that particular resource. Non-living renewable natural resources include dirt and water.

Flow renewable resources are very much like renewable resources, only they do not need regeneration, unlike renewable resources. Flow renewable resources include renewable energy sources such as the following renewable power sources: solar, geothermal, landfill gas, tides and wind.

Resources can also be classified on the basis of their origin as biotic and abiotic. Biotic resources are derived from living organisms. Abiotic resources are derived from the non-living world (e.g., land, water, and air). Mineral and power resources can be abiotic natural resources.

Non-renewable Resources

A non-renewable resource is a natural resource that exists in a fixed amount that cannot be re-made, re-grown or regenerated as fast as it is consumed and used up.

Some non-renewable resources can be renewable but take an extremely long time to renew. Fossil fuels, for example, take millions of years to form and so are not practically considered 'renewable'. Different non-renewable resources like oil, coal, natural gas etc. have different levels of demand from different sectors like transportation and residences with each resource specializing for each sector. Many environmentalists propose a tax on consumption of non renewable resources. Non-renewable resources cannot be replaced or can only be replaced over thousands or millions of years.

Natural Capital

Natural resources are natural capital converted to commodity inputs to infrastructural capital processes They include soil, timber, oil, minerals, and other goods harvested from the Earth. Both extraction of the basic resource and refining it into a purer, directly usable form, (e.g., metals, refined oils) are generally considered natural-resource activities, even though the latter may not necessarily occur near the former. This process generates high profits due to the high demand for the natural resources and the energies that they are able to generate.

A nation's natural resources often determine its wealth in the world economic system and its diplomatic, military, and political influence. Developed nations are those which are less dependent on natural resources for wealth, due to their greater reliance on infrastructural capital for production. However, some see a resource curse whereby easily obtainable natural resources could actually hurt the prospects of a national economy by fostering political corruption. Political corruption can negatively impact the national economy because time is spent giving bribes or other economically unproductive acts instead of the generation of generative economic activity. This has been seen over the years with legislation passed to appease companies who will benefit. There also tends to be concentrations of ownership over specific plots of land that have proven to yield natural resources.

In recent years, the depletion of natural capital and attempts to move to sustainable development have been a major focus of development agencies. This is of particular concern in rainforest regions, which hold most of the Earth's natural biodiversity - irreplaceable genetic natural capital. Conservation of natural resources is the major focus of natural capitalism, environmentalism, the ecology movement, and green politics. Some view this depletion as a major source of social unrest and conflicts in developing nations.

Renewable Energy

Solar energy is the energy derived directly from the Sun. Along with nuclear energy, it is the most abundant source of energy on Earth. The fastest growing type of alternative energy increasing at 50 percent a year, is the photovoltaic cell, which converts sunlight directly into electricity. The Sun yearly delivers more than 10,000 times the energy that humans currently use.

Wind power is derived from uneven heating of the Earth's surface from the Sun and the warm core. Most modern wind power is generated in the form of electricity by converting the rotation of turbine blades into electrical current by means of an electrical generator. In windmills (a much older technology) wind energy is used to turn mechanical machinery to do physical work, like crushing grain or pumping water.

Hydropower is energy derived from the movement of water in rivers and oceans (or other energy differentials), can likewise be used to generate electricity using turbines, or can be used mechanically to do useful work. It is a very common resource.

Geothermal power directly harnesses the natural flow of heat from the ground. The available energy from natural decay of radioactive elements in the earths, crust, and mantle is approximately equal to that of incoming solar energy, especially during the day.

Alcohol derived from corn, sugar cane, switchgrass, etc. is also a renewable source of energy. Similarly, oils from plants and seeds can be used as a substitute for non-renewable diesel. Methane is also considered as a renewable source of energy.

Nuclear power, particularly a breeder reactor, is often considered Agricultural products.

Techniques in agriculture which allow for minimal or controlled environmental damage qualify as sustainable agriculture. Products (foods, chemicals, biofuels, etc) from this type of agriculture may be considered "sustainable" when processing, logistics, etc. also have sustainable characteristics.

Similarly, forest products such as lumber, plywood, paper and chemicals, can be renewable resources when produced by sustainable forestry techniques.

Water

Water can qualify as a renewable material (also non-renewable) when carefully controlled usage, treatment, and release are followed. If not, it would become a non-renewable resource at that location. For example, groundwater could be removed from an aquifer at a rate greater than the sustainable recharge. Removal of water from the pore spaces may cause permanent compaction (subsidence) that cannot be renewed.

Geothermal Power

Geothermal power (from the Greek roots *geo*, meaning earth, and *thermos*, meaning heat) is energy generated from heat stored in the earth, or the collection of absorbed heat derived from underground.

Prince Piero Ginori Conti tested the first geothermal generator on 4 July 1904, at the Larderello dry steam field in Italy. The largest group of geothermal power plants in the world is located at The Geysers, a geothermal field in California, United States. The Philippines and Iceland are the only countries to generate a significant percentage of their electricity from geothermal sources; in both countries 15-20% of power comes from geothermal plants. As of 2008, geothermal power supplies less than 1% of the world's energy. The most common type of geothermal power plants (binary plants) are closed cycle operations and release essentially no Greenhouse gas emissions; geothermal power is available 24 hours a day with average availabilities above 90% (compared to about 75% for coal plants).

Geothermal Technologies

Geothermal resources range from shallow ground to hot water and rock several kilometres below the Earth's surface, and even further down to the extremely hot molten rock called magma. Wells over 1.5 km deep can be drilled into underground reservoirs to tap steam and very hot water that can be brought to the surface for use in a variety of applications.

Geothermal technologies include:

- Binary cycle power plants, which pass moderately hot geothermal water by a secondary fluid with a much lower boiling point than water. This causes the secondary fluid to flash to vapor, which then drives the turbines. This is the most common type of geothermal, both ORC and Kalina cycles are used.
- Hot dry rock geothermal energy: Using deep wells into hot rock, a fluid is heated and used to generate power. Also known as EGS or Enhanced Geothermal Systems.
- Dry steam plants, which directly use geothermal steam to turn turbines;
- Flash steam plants, which pull deep, high-pressure hot water into lower-pressure tanks and use the resulting flashed steam to drive turbines; and
- Direct heat: Hot water near Earth's surface can be piped directly into facilities and used to heat buildings, grow plants in greenhouses, dehydrate onions and garlic, heat water for fish farming, and pasteurize milk. Some cities pipe the hot water under roads and pavements to melt snow. District heating applications use networks of piped hot water to heat buildings in whole communities.

A geothermal heat pump system consists of pipes buried in the shallow ground near a building, a heat exchanger, and ductwork into the building. In winter, heat from the relatively warmer ground goes through the heat exchanger into the house. In summer, hot air from the house is pulled through the heat exchanger into the relatively cooler ground. Heat removed during the summer can be used as no-cost energy to heat water.

Direct exchange geothermal heat pump: A heat pump without a heat exchanger, which circulates the working fluid through pipes in the ground.

Advantages

Krafla Geothermal Station in northeast Iceland Geothermal power requires no fuel, and is therefore virtually emissions free and insusceptible to fluctuations in fuel cost. And because a geothermal power station doesn't rely on transient sources of energy, unlike, for example, wind turbines or solar panels, its capacity factor can be quite large; up to 90% in practice.

It is considered to be sustainable because the heat extraction is small compared to the size of the heat reservoir. While individual wells may need to recover, geothermal heat is inexhaustible and is replenished from greater depths. The long-term sustainability of geothermal energy production has been demonstrated at the Lardarello field in Italy since 1913, at the Wairakei field in New Zealand since 1958, and at The Geysers field in California since 1960.

Geothermal has minimal land use requirements; existing geothermal plants use 1-8 acres per megawatt (MW) versus 5-10 acres per MW for nuclear operations and 19 acres per MW for coal power plants It also offers a degree of scalability: a large geothermal plant can power entire cities while smaller power plants can supply more remote sites such as rural villages.

Disadvantages

From an engineering perspective, the geothermal fluid is corrosive and, worse, is at a low temperature compared to steam from boilers. By the laws of thermodynamics this low temperature limits the efficiency of heat engines in extracting useful energy during the generation of electricity. Much of the heat energy is lost, unless there is also a local use for low-temperature heat such as greenhouses, timber mills, and district heating. However, since this energy is almost free once the plant is established, the efficiency of the system is not as significant as for a coal or other powered plant.

There are several environmental concerns behind geothermal energy. Construction of the power plants can adversely affect land stability in the surrounding region. This is mainly a concern with Enhanced Geothermal Systems, where water is injected into hot dry rock where no water was before. Dry steam and flash steam power plants also emit low levels of carbon dioxide, nitric oxide, and sulphur, although at roughly 5% of the levels emitted by fossil fuel power plants. However, geothermal plants can be built with emissions-controlling systems that can inject these substances back into the earth, thereby reducing carbon emissions to less than 0.1% of those from fossil fuel power plants. Hot water from geothermal sources will contain trace amounts of dangerous elements such as mercury, arsenic, and antimony which, if disposed of into rivers, can render their water unsafe to drink.

Although geothermal sites are capable of providing heat for many decades, locations may eventually cool down. For example, the world's second-oldest geothermal generator at Wairakei has reduced production. It is likely that locations like these were designed too large for the site, since there is only so much energy that can be stored and replenished in a given volume of earth. If left alone, however, these places should recover their lost heat, as the Earth's mantle and core have vast heat reserves. Geothermal and biomass are the only two renewable resources which must be carefully managed in order to avoid local depletion. An assessment of the total potential for electricity production from the high-temperature geothermal fields in Iceland gives a value of about 1500 TWh (total) or 15 TWh per year over a 100 year period. The electricity production capacity from geothermal fields is now only 1.3 TWh per year.

Potential

At pesent, only a small percentage of the total potential power is effectively used if heat recovered by ground source heat pumps is included, the non-electric generating capacity of geothermal energy is estimated at more than 100 GW (gigawatts of thermal power) in the United States, while there were also plants under construction in 11 other countries.

According to a 1999 study, it was thought that this might amount to between 65 and 138 GW of electrical generation capacity 'using enhanced technology'.

- 1 billion US dollars in research and development over 15 years.
- improvements - sufficient to provide all the world's present energy needs for several millennia.

The key characteristic of an EGS (also called a Hot Dry Rock system), is that it reaches at least 10 km down into hard rock. At a typical site two holes would be bored and the deep rock between them fractured. Water would be pumped down one and steam would come up the other. The MIT report estimated that there was enough energy in hard rocks 10 km below the United States to supply all the world's current needs for 30,000.

Drilling at this depth is now possible in the petroleum industry, altough it is an expensive process. For example, Exxon has announced an 11-kilometre (7 mi) hole at the Chayvo field, SakhalinWells drilled to depths greater than 4 kilometres (2 mi) generally incur drilling costs in the tens of millions of dollars. The technological challenges are to drill wide bores at low cost and to break rock over larger volumes. Apart from the energy used to make the bores, the process releases no greenhouse gases.

Other important countries considered high in potential for development are the People's Republic of China, Hungary,

Mexico, Iceland, and New Zealand. A number of potential sites are being developed or evaluated in South Australia that are several kilometres in depth.

History of Development

Extraction of geothermal power has been limited to the edges of tectonic plates. Geothermal steam and hot springs have been used for centuries for bathing and heating, but it was not until the 20th century that geothermal power started being used to make electricity.

Prince Piero Ginori Conti tested the first geothermal power generator on 4 July 1904, at the Larderello dry steam field in Italy. It was a small generator that lit four light bulbs Later, in 1911, the world's first geothermal power plant was built there. It was the world's only industrial producer of geothermal electricity until 1958, when New Zealand built a plant of its own.

The first geothermal power plant in the United States was made in 1922 by John D. Grant at The Geysers Resort Hotel. After drilling for more steam, he was able to generate enough electricity to light the entire resort. Eventually the power plant fell into disuse, as it was not competitive with other methods of energy production.

In 1960, Pacific Gas and Electric began operation of the first successful geothermal power plant in the United States at The Geysers. The original turbine installed lasted for more than 30 years and produced 11 MW net power. The Geysers are currently owned by the Calpine Corporation and the Northern California Power Agency. They currently produce over 750 MW of power.

Development Around the World

Geothermal power is generated in over 20 countries around the world including the United States, Iceland, Italy, Germany, Turkey, France, The Netherlands, Lithuania,

New Zealand, Mexico, El Salvador, Nicaragua, Costa Rica, Russia, the Philippines, Indonesia, the People's Republic of China, Japan and Saint Kitts and Nevis. Chevron Corporation is the world's largest producer of geothermal energy. Other companies as Reykjavik Energy Invest also help other countries of setting up geothermal energy plants.

Australia

Geothermal energy is only in the exploration and development stage in Australia and not yet a source of usable electrical power.

Canada

Canada's government (which officially notes some 30,000 earth-heat installations for providing space heating to Canadian residential and commercial buildings) reports that the most advanced project exists as a test geothermal-electrical site in the Meager Mountain-Pebble Creek area of British Columbia, where a 100-300 MW facility could be developed.

The remaining Canadian provinces and territories contain potential for Enhanced Geothermal. Low temperature - or direct heat potential (sometimes called geothermal heating) exist everywhere in Canada.

Denmark

Denmark has two geothermal power plants, one in Thisted started in 1988, and one in Copenhagen started in 2005.

Germany

Electricity from geothermal sources is expected to grow in Germany mainly because a law that benefits the production of geothermal electricity and guarantees a feed-in tariff. Less than 0.4 percent of Germany's total primary energy supply came from geothermal sources in 2004. But after a renewable energy law that introduced a tariff scheme of EU 0.15 [US $0.23] per kilowatt-hour (kWh) for electricity produced from geothermal sources came into effect that year, a construction boom was sparked and the new power plants are now starting to come online. However the first German geothermal power plant had been build in 2003 in Neustadt-Glewe located in northern Germany. This plant was not just the first one operating with the ORC-technology Organic Rankine Cycle but also with the lowest temperature.

This first project proved that the generation of electricity from geothermal sources on low temperature levels is possible in Germany. In the same year the TAB (bureau for technological impact assessment of the German Bundestag) concluded that Germany's geothermal resources could be used to supply the entire base load of the country. A conclusion that had been made regarding the fact that geothermal sources have to be developed sustainably because they can cool out if overused.

Ice land

Ice land is situated in an area with a high concentration of volcanoes, making it an ideal location for generating geothermal energy. 19.1% of Iceland's electrical energy is generated from geothermal sources In addition, geothermal heating is used to heat 87% of homes in Iceland. Icelanders plan to be 100% fossil fuel-free in the near future.

Kenya

Geothermal power is very cost-effective in the Rift area of Kenya, Africa. Kenya was the first African country to build geothermal energy sources. Kenya's KenGen has built two plants, Olkaria I (45 MW) and Olkaria II (65 MW), with a third private plant Olkaria III (48 MW). Plans are to increase production capacity by another 576 MW by 2017, covering 25% of Kenya's electricity needs, and correspondingly reducing dependency on imported oil. In

Ethiopia there is another plant for geothermal power (in 2008 some experts from Iceland calculated that Ethiopia has at least 1000 MW of that energy). Hot spots have been found across the continent, especially in the Great Rift Valley.

Mexico

Mexico has the third greatest geothermal energy production with an installed capacity of 959.50 MW by December 2007. This represents 3.24% of the total electricity generated in the country.

United States

The West Ford Flat power plant is one of 21 power plants at the Geysers, the United States of America is the country with the greatest geothermal energy production.

The largest dry steam field in the world is The Geysers, 116 km (72 miles) north of San Francisco. The Geysers began in 1960, has 1360 MW of installed capacity and produces over 750 MW net. Calpine Corporation now owns 19 of the 21 plants in The Geysers and is currently the United States' largest producer of geothermal energy. The other two plants are owned jointly by the Northern California Power Agency and the City of Santa Clara's municipal Electric Utility (now called Silicon Valley Power). Since the activities of one geothermal plant affects those nearby, the consolidation plant ownership at The Geysers has been beneficial because the plants operate cooperatively instead of in their own short-term interest. The Geysers is now recharged by injecting treated sewage effluent from the City of Santa Rosa and the Lake County sewage treatment plant. This sewage effluent used to be dumped into rivers and streams and is now piped to the geothermal field where it replenishes the steam produced for power generation.

Another major geothermal area is located in south central California, on the southeast side of the Salton Sea, near the cities of Niland and Calipatria, California. As of 2001, there were 15 geothermal plants producing electricity in the area. CalEnergy owns about half of them and the rest are owned by various companies. Combined the plants have a capacity of about 570 MW.

The Basin and Range geologic province in Nevada, southeastern Oregon, southwestern Idaho, Arizona and western Utah is now an area of rapid geothermal development. Several small power plants were built during the late 1980s during times of high power prices. Rising energy costs have spurred new development. Plants in Nevada at Steamboat near Reno, Brady/Desert Peak, Dixie Valley, Soda Lake, Stillwater and Beowawe now produce about 235 MW.

13

Chemical Reaction

A chemical reaction is a process that always results in the interconversion of chemical substances. The substance or substances initially involved in a chemical reaction are called reactants. Chemical reactions are usually characterized by a chemical change, and they yield one or more products, which usually have properties different from the reactants. Classically, chemical reactions encompass changes that strictly involve the motion of electrons in the forming and breaking of chemical bonds, although the general concept of a chemical reaction, in particular the notion of a chemical equation, is applicable to transformations of elementary particles, as well as nuclear reactions.

Different chemical reactions are used in combination in chemical synthesis in order to get a desired product. In biochemistry, series of chemical reactions catalyzed by enzymes form metabolic pathways, by which syntheses and decompositions ordinarily impossible in conditions within a cell are performed.

Reaction Types

The large diversity of chemical reactions and approaches to their study results in the existence of several concurring, often overlapping, ways of classifying them. Below are examples of widely used terms for describing common kinds of reactions.

- *Isomerisation*, in which a chemical compound undergoes a structural rearrangement without any change in its net atomic composition; see stereoisomerism.
- *Direct combination or synthesis*, in which 2 or more chemical elements or compounds unite to form a more complex product:

  $N_2 + 3\ H_2 \rightarrow 2\ NH_3$
- *Chemical decomposition* or analysis, in which a compound is decomposed into smaller compounds or elements:

  $2\ H_2O \rightarrow 2\ H_2 + O_2$
- *Single displacement* or substitution, characterized by an element being displaced out of a compound by a more reactive element:

  $2\ Na(s) + 2\ HCl(aq) \rightarrow 2\ NaCl(aq) + H_2(g)$
- *Metathesis or Double displacement reaction*, in which two compounds exchange ions or bonds to form different compounds:

  $NaCl(aq) + AgNO_3(aq) \rightarrow NaNO_3(aq) + AgCl(s)$
- *Acid-base* reactions, broadly characterized as reactions between an acid and a base, can have different definitions depending on the acid-base concept employed. Some of the most common are:
  - *Arrhenius definition:* Acids dissociate in water releasing H_3O^+ ions; bases dissociate in water releasing OH- ions.
  - *Brønsted-Lowry definition:* Acids are proton (H^+) donors; bases are proton acceptors. Includes the Arrhenius definition.

- *Lewis definition:* Acids are electron-pair acceptors; bases are electron-pair donors. Includes the Brønsted-Lowry definition.

- *Redox reactions,* in which changes in *oxidation numbers* of atoms in involved species occur. Those reactions can often be interpreted as transferences of electrons between different molecular sites or species. An example of a redox reaction is:

  $2\ S_2O_3^{2-}(aq) + I_2(aq) \rightarrow S_4O_6^{2-}(aq) + 2\ I^-(aq)$

  In which I_2 is reduced to I^- and $S_2O_3^{2-}$ (thiosulfate anion) is oxidized to $S_4O_6^{2-}$.

- *Combustion,* a kind of redox reaction in which any combustible substance combines with an oxidizing element, usually oxygen, to generate heat and form oxidized products. The term combustion is usually used for only large-scale oxidation of whole molecules, i.e. a controlled oxidation of a single functional group is not combustion.

  $C_{10}H_8 + 12\ O_2 \rightarrow 10\ CO_2 + 4\ H_2O$

  $CH_2S + 6\ F_2 \rightarrow CF_4 + 2\ HF + SF_6$

- *Disproportionation* with one reactant forming two distinct products varying in oxidation state.

  $2\ Sn^{2+} \rightarrow Sn + Sn^{4+}$

Organic reactions encompass a wide assortment of reactions involving compounds which have carbon as the main element in their molecular structure. The reactions in which an organic compound may take part are largely defined by its functional groups.

Chemical Kinetics

The rate of a chemical reaction is a measure of how the concentration or pressure of the involved substances changes with time. Analysis of reaction rates is important for several applications, such as in chemical engineering or in chemical equilibrium study. Rates of reaction depends basically on:

- *Reactant concentrations*, which usually make the reaction happen at a faster rate if raised through increased collisions per unit time.
- *Surface area* available for contact between the reactants, in particular solid ones in heterogeneous systems. Larger surface area leads to higher reaction rates.
- *Pressure*, by increasing the pressure, you decrease the volume between molecules. This will increase the frequency of collisions of molecules.
- *Activation energy*, which is defined as the amount of energy required to make the reaction start and carry on spontaneously. Higher activation energy implies that the reactants need more energy to start than a reaction with a lower activation energy.
- *Temperature*, which hastens reactions if raised, since higher temperature increases the energy of the molecules, creating more collisions per unit time.
- The presence or absence of a *catalyst*. Catalysts are substances which change the pathway (mechanism) of a reaction which in turn increases the speed of a reaction by lowering the activation energy needed for the reaction to take place. A catalyst is not destroyed or changed during a reaction, so it can be used again.
- For some reactions, the presence of *electromagnetic radiation*, most notably ultraviolet, is needed to promote the breaking of bonds to start the reaction. This is particularly true for reactions involving radicals.

Reaction rates are related to the concentrations of substances involved in reactions, as quantified by the rate law of each reaction. Note that some reactions have rates that are independent of reactant concentrations. These are called zero order reactions.

Reactions and Energy

Chemical energy is part of all chemical reactions. Energy is needed to break chemical bonds in the starting substances. As new bonds form in the final substances, energy is released. By comparing the chemical energy of the original substances with the chemical energy of the final substances, you can decide if energy is released or absorbed in the overall reaction.

Exothermic Reactions

A chemical reaction in which energy is released is called an exothermic reaction. Exo means "go out" or "exit." *Thermic* means "heat" or "energy." Exothermic reactions can give off energy in several forms. If heat is released in an exothermic reaction, the nearby matter will become warmer. The nearby matter absorbs the heat released by the reaction. The reaction between gasoline and oxygen in a car's engine is an exothermic reaction.

Index

D

E

❑❑❑